GW01081173

Following in Your Footsteps:

How to Pass On Your Faith to Your Children

Adapted by
Stephen and Amanda Sorenson

Heritage Builders

FOLLOWING IN YOUR FOOTSTEPS
HOW TO PASS ON YOUR FAITH TO YOUR CHILDREN
Copyright © 2002, Focus on the Family. All rights reserved.
International copyright secured.

Library of Congress Cataloging-in-Publication Data
Sorenson, Stephen.
    Following in your footsteps : building a spiritual heritage at
home / Stephen and Amanda Sorenson.
        p. cm.
    ISBN 1-58997-064-0
    1. Christian education—Home training. I. Sorenson, Amanda, 1953-
II. Title.
    BV1590 .S69 2001
    248.8`45—dc21
                    2001005539

Published by Focus on the Family.

Text adapted by: Stephen and Amanda Sorenson. Colorado Springs, CO
Cover design: Peak Creative
Interior design: Angela Barnes

Printed in the United States of America

    03 04 05/ 10 9 8 7 6 5 4 3

Contents

SESSION ONE: *Your Most Important Calling* 1
Just Try It! Activities 9
Discussion Questions 12

SESSION TWO: *Spiritual Training Is Not Optional* 15
Just Try It! Activities 25
Discussion Questions 28

SESSION THREE: *The Legacy You Got, the Legacy You
Can Give* 29
Emotional Legacy Evaluation 31
Social Legacy Evaluation 34
Spiritual Legacy Evaluation 36
Designing Your Heritage 40
Heritage Evaluation 43
Just Try It! Activities 45
Discussion Questions 48

SESSION FOUR: *Creating Family Fragrance* 51
Just Try It! Activities 61
Discussion Questions 63

SESSION FIVE: *The Influence of Family Traditions, Family
Compass, and Teachable Moments* 65
Family Creed Worksheet 81
Just Try It! Activities 82
Discussion Questions 85

SESSION SIX: *Tailoring Your Spiritual Growth Plan to*
                Your Unique Family 87
                Just Try It! Activities 97
                Discussion Questions 100

APPENDIX: *How to Lead Your Child to Christ* 101

                Notes 104

Your Most Important Calling

*"These commandments that I give you today are to
be upon your hearts. Impress them on your children.
Talk about them when you sit at home and when you walk
along the road, when you lie down and when you get up."*
(DEUTERONOMY 6:6-7)

One rainy August morning, two young adventurers decided to scale Mount Dom, a 14,942-foot peak near Zermatt, Switzerland. About noon, they started hiking up the forested trail, planning to spend the night in a small, heated hut halfway up the mountain.

It was raining and the temperature soon started to drop. Wishing they had brought cold weather gear, they kept going. At 6:00 P.M. the rain turned to snow. Now well above timberline, they were having a hard time following the trail.

Two hours later, chilled to the bone and wandering around in pitch black darkness, both of them knew they were in serious trouble. With no tent or sleeping bags, they couldn't escape the elements. They knew they might die from hypothermia.

Suddenly they saw a tiny, flickering light far away. With renewed hope, they hurried toward it and were saved. Why did the light suddenly appear? The keeper of the "high hut" decided to hang a kerosene lamp by the door—just in case.[1]

This story, in many ways, captures the essence of this short book.

Our children begin the journey of life with high hopes, naive to the fact that they are heading into the gathering darkness of a sinful world. On their own, even if they are armed with lots of self-confidence and youthful vitality, they face a world that is growing ever colder to the claims of Jesus.

Those two climbers needed that kerosene lamp to guide them to safety, and they needed someone who was willing to place it where it could be seen. That is our role as Christian parents. We have the privilege, and the calling, to place Jesus— the "Light of the World"—in front of our children. He alone can guide them, save them, and shelter them from the world's storms—now and forever.

Parenting is a high, holy, and costly calling. God gifts us with our children to love, nurture, and teach. Then He asks us to release them to Him and trust Him to complete the work we have started in their lives—to surrender to Him what we hold most dear.

But how do you—a parent or grandparent—"hang up the lamp"? How do you keep it burning brightly? How do you help children learn to successfully navigate life's threatening storms?

> **You probably already do more than you realize to guide your children into a deeper understanding of God!**

The good news is, you probably already do more than you realize to guide your children into a deeper understanding of God. You realize how important parenting is. And even though you may not *feel* qualified to be more intentional about passing along the Christian faith to your children, you already have what it takes.

That's what this book is all about. We want to help you capitalize on activities you already do with your child(ren)—and give you some new ideas that have been "field tested" by other parents.

Guiding your children doesn't have to be intimidating. In fact, it can be lots of fun for everyone! And as you'll see, it requires little preparation time. You can do effective spiritual training in as little as an hour a week with the whole family and a few minutes of one-on-one time with each child five days a week.

WHAT'S YOUR SITUATION?

Read through the following list and check the statements that apply to you.

___ I am trying to raise at least one child to know Christ and come to accept the biblical values I hold dear. I have questions about how to do that effectively.

___ I know I ought to be more intentional in teaching my children Bible-based truth, but I am not sure what or how to teach.

___ I am busy and juggling many responsibilities.

___ I see changes taking place in our culture, and I would like to prepare my children for the many challenges and issues they soon will face.

___ I wish that when I was growing up someone had modeled what it meant to provide spiritual training, so I'd have a better idea of how to provide that for my children.

___ I am parenting alone.

___ I have children of different ages.

___ I feel inadequate.

___ I have a child with special needs.

___ I have already tried something like this and it didn't work.

___ I am a bit shaky in my spiritual life.

___ I don't know a lot about the Bible.

If you are like most people with whom we interact, you checked at least four of these statements. Be encouraged! You are not alone. Many parents who face these same issues and questions have already discovered how easy it is to begin laying a spiritual foundation for their children.

You—the "Mommy," "Daddy," "Papa," or "Nana"—have been thrust into the most important role of your life. You have the chance to positively influence future generations in ways you can't even imagine. No pressure, right?

So, we'd like to assist you in six key ways:

Help you use an effective, simple, and proven plan for guiding your children into deeper spiritual growth and a vibrant relationship with God through Jesus Christ.

Encourage, Equip, and **Empower** you to successfully start using this plan *today*.

Guide you in engaging your children in fun activities that your children will enjoy—activities that will keep them motivated to learn.

Introduce you to the stories of other parents who are seeing the exciting benefits of intentionally teaching biblical truths to their children.

In these six easy-to-use sessions, we'll give you a number of hints, insights, Scripture references, practical tips, and ideas. Starting today, you can experience the joy that comes from seeing your children grow closer to God. It'll only take about an hour per session to lay a strong spiritual foundation for family learning that can last for many years.

You don't have to be a teacher, Bible scholar, or seminary professor to teach your children important biblical truths. What's important is that you get started and have a plan. Having a plan is important because the rest of the world wants to reach your kids with its own plan—and it's certainly not a God-centered one!

> **"It is never too late to make an eternal difference in the life of your child. . . . Look forward to all the opportunities you have to do something with your family."**
> —CAROL KUYKENDALL

It's never too late to start planting spiritual concepts in the minds and hearts of your children. And it's not as hard as you might think. You can teach spiritual truths when putting your kids to bed. Or while you ride in a car together. Or during mealtimes, movie times, game times, vacation times . . . almost any time you are together as a family.

As parents, we don't need to figure out all the possible ways to "train a child in the way he should go" (Proverbs 22:6). Rather, we need to concentrate on taking one step at a time in the right direction, allowing God to lead us and our children down the paths He has chosen.

Today you are starting an adventure that will lead to wonderful benefits. Teaching spiritual truth to your children —teaching them to know, love, and serve Jesus—can be fun, exciting, and most of all, life-changing.

Tip
Always Take a Kid Along
"Hey, Jake. Put your shoes on. Let's get going."

"Okay, Dad."

It's Saturday: errand day for Dad. The van needs an oil change. A trip to the hardware store for screws and pipes and gadgets for the latest home improvement project. The perfect time for a one-on-one with one of the kids.

My dad taught me that. "Never go anywhere without a

child," he told me. And he's right. By taking a kid away from the siblings, I get his or her full attention, and the child gets mine. I'm building the relationship while setting up the impromptu times. . . . The principle is that I must develop the relationship, for the relationship gives me the ability to share spiritual truth.   —J. W.[2]

 Points to Ponder
Think about what you are doing, or have done already, to guide your child into deeper faith in Christ. These may include:

- Saying a prayer before a meal or at bedtime.
- Attending a local church with your child.
- Reading Christian books aloud.
- Answering questions about Jesus.
- Emphasizing that the Bible is God's Word.

PROVIDING AN INTERNAL GUIDING LINE

Years ago, a 15-year-old swimmer named Johnny Weissmuller was winning every race in his "home" pool—because he could watch the black tile stripes marking his lane and swim in a straight line. But whenever he'd swim races in other pools that had no lane lines, he'd lose. He had come to depend on the clearly marked lines in his home pool to keep him on a straight course. Without them, he wobbled all over and used up precious time and energy.

So Johnny's coach, William Bachrach, placed his hat at the other end of a pool that had no lane lines and said, "That hat is your goal. Fix it in your mind, draw a mental line to it, and swim for it." Johnny did, and from that time on he carried his own "lines" in his head whenever he raced in an unmarked pool.

Eventually Johnny became the first Tarzan in the movies—after winning five Olympic medals during two Olympic Games![3]

We may do our best to give our children guidelines to follow, and our children may do well when they are in the security of our homes and the lines are clear and well marked. But times have changed. Whereas 50 years ago there were still commonly understood "lines" of biblically based standards painted on the bottom of every "pool," these don't exist today. (In fact, the word translated "righteousness" in the Bible means "to stay within the lines.") Our children soon discover that there are no bold, well-marked lines of behavior or commitment. There is little to steer children away from problems or keep them from drifting out of bounds. Today's "swimming pools" are muddied by sin. Many people believe there are no absolute lines of truth—only situational ethics and standards that change all the time. You can begin helping your children learn the "mental lines" they will need to carry with them in order to face the challenges of life as they grow closer to God.

 ### Questions

- Why is it important to give our children "mental lines" that will keep them away from problems and enable them to win the race of living a godly life?
- Why do children need moral and ethical boundaries that don't change based on opinion polls?
- How do you feel about trying to help your children establish the "mental lines" they need? Excited? A little afraid? Why?

 ### Points to Ponder

Spiritual training is not an add-on; it forms the core of your children's being and life. With your help, they can be equipped to not only cope in today's world but to make a significant difference for the kingdom of God. They need to know the truths and principles that explain and govern life.

As we all know, any learning process requires theory (instruction) and practical training. You can read a book about how to play baseball or have someone explain the rules to you, but until someone physically shows you how to play the game and you start practicing, everything you know is just theory.

As parents, we are to teach our children about God and the Christian life *and* show them by example and training how to live it out. So we need to be teachable, to allow God to parent us. We need God's filling. We have to seek ways in which we can dig deeper in our faith and draw closer to God. As we read the Bible and spend time with God in prayer, God will provide what we need so that we, in turn, will have something to pass on to our children.

Potential Benefits to Your Children of Spiritual Training

- Eternal life through a personal relationship with Jesus.
- An ongoing, loving relationship with God.
- God's guidance, wisdom, and direction for their lives, as well as His discipline, correction, and forgiveness when they make mistakes.
- God's help during difficult times.
- Purpose and a sense of value through knowing that God created them uniquely, loves them, and has a special plan for each of their lives.
- A strong understanding of right and wrong.
- An understanding of principles governing interpersonal relationships so they can develop healthy relationships with others.
- Thankful hearts, teachable spirits, strong morals, and a desire for personal growth.

Just Try It!

In each session, we'll provide activities you can do with your children. Be sure to do the activity marked with this symbol  with your children today. It's an "assignment" of sorts—but one you and your family will grow to appreciate. Get started right now and start discovering the benefits of this easy plan.

To add options, we've provided other activities from which to choose. Make choices based on the time you have available and the ages of your children. Through prayer, patience, and an intentional plan, you can become a successful spiritual trainer in your home and make a difference—one precious life at a time!

"What Do You Know About God?" *(5-10 minutes, all ages)*
At bedtime (for younger children) or a time when things have quieted down a little, ask each child to share with you some things he or she knows about God. Be prepared to share a few things yourself, too. (For example: God is the Creator. He is loving and kind. He hates sin. He wants to have a personal relationship with each of us. He listens to our prayers. If your child is older, explore more advanced issues, such as God's character and why it's important for us to know what He is like.)

Prayer *(1 minute, all ages)*
Say a mealtime prayer, thanking God that He is with us in all situations and guiding and directing our lives.

Bible Game *(15 minutes, more advanced)*
One person thinks of a place, person, or thing mentioned in the Bible—and keeps it a secret. Other family members ask

questions that require yes or no answers and try to figure out
what the person is thinking of. Everyone can ask up to 20
questions to try to guess the answer. Then someone else can
think of a place, person, or thing. *[Example: Mom might think of
Noah's ark, by which Noah's family and all the animals were saved
from the great flood.]*

✹ "Directions" Game *(10 minutes, up to age 12)*

Say: "Let's pretend a new friend calls and wants to know
how to get to _____ *[choose a special place where you live—
a great ice cream store, a swimming pool, a fun restaurant, a minia-
ture golf place, and so on]*. Which landmarks would you
mention? What would you use to give instructions?"

After discussion about directions, say: "God has an even
better treasure to share with us—the directions He gives us in
the Bible. There He tells us what He is like and how to get to
know Him better. He tells us how to get along with people,
how to pray, how to get to heaven, and much more. And His
directions are always right and perfect for each of us!"

Then read Psalm 119:89-90: "Your word, O LORD, is eternal; it stands firm in the heavens. Your faithfulness continues
through all generations."

Say: "The Bible—God's Word—doesn't get outdated as
time passes. The words in the Bible have come from God and
will last forever. But we can choose whether to pay attention
to what God says or to follow the words and teachings of
someone else. Why do you think it's important for us to read
God's Word and do what it says?"

✹ Create a Refrigerator Plaque *(15 minutes, up to age 10)*

Materials needed: sheet of large paper (bigger than
8½"x 11"), crayons or colored pencils, Bible, piece of tape.

Invite your children to sit at a table. Say: "There are many
great verses in the Bible. I'd like us to use one to make a special reminder that we can put on the refrigerator." Look up

Joshua 24:15 and read this verse aloud: "As for me and my household, we will serve the LORD."

Write out those words from the verse on the paper and invite the children to decorate it. As you decorate, talk about what it means to serve the Lord. [*Obeying Him. Wanting to do what He wants you to do. Spending time with Him in prayer. Telling other people about Him.*]

After the decorating is done, tape the verse on the refrigerator door.

Discussion Questions

The following questions are designed to stimulate discussion in a small-group setting such as a neighborhood Bible study, Sunday school class, or parenting class. We encourage you to listen to the audiotape for each session as a group before discussing the questions, but you may choose to use only this book if your group time is quite limited. It would be best if everyone in your group has the book and is excited about using it with their children.

Let's Talk About It

• What have we already been doing, as parents or grandparents, to help our children learn more about God and the Bible? (For example: Taking our children to church. Reading Bible stories to them. Praying before meals.)

• What are some reasons why many Christian parents and grandparents do not intentionally plant spiritual concepts in the minds of their children or grandchildren?

• Why do our children need a strong spiritual foundation?

• Do we feel competent in trying to help our children learn more about God and the Bible? Why or why not?

• What can we do, as parents and grandparents, to demonstrate to our children our love for God and desire to know Him better?

• Why is it important for us to start teaching our children and grandchildren today instead of putting it off until a more convenient time?

• Do you agree or disagree with this statement: "Spiritual training is not an add-on; it forms the core of our children's being and life"? Why?

- What does it mean to "share the light of Jesus" with our children? What does that look like, in practical terms?
- Deuteronomy 6:6-7 says, "These commandments that I give you today are to be upon your hearts. Impress them on your children. Talk about them when you sit at home and when you walk along the road, when you lie down and when you get up." When you hear these verses, what do you think? What do you feel?

Spiritual Training Is Not Optional

*"Train a child in the way he should go,
and when he is old he will not turn from it."*
(PROVERBS 22:6)

Nearly two years old, talkative Trevor was sweet, mild mannered, and obedient. At a friend's house, his mother chatted while Trevor sat on the edge of the pool. His chubby feet dangled in the cool water while the adults laughed and told stories. Mom kept a careful eye on him.

Suddenly a belligerent bee flew into the group, landing on people. The adults stood up, and Mom turned her back on Trevor to swat at the bee with a sandal. When she turned around, Trevor was floating facedown in the water.

Alerted by Mom's cry, another woman leaped to the pool and pulled Trevor out of the water.

After much sputtering and coughing, Trevor told them that he had reached for a ball that had fallen into the pool. But he reached too far and simply, quietly slipped into the water. "I was calling you, Mommy," Trevor said, "but you didn't hear me. You didn't come get me."

Mom cried as she held her little boy. *I only had my back to the pool for a few seconds,* she thought. *Only seconds. And if I had not spun around when I did, he might have drowned.*

Certainly after this incident Mom realized how important it was for Trevor to receive swimming lessons. If he had even completed a beginner's class, he could have paddled to the side of the pool.

Yes, it will be a hassle sometimes for Mom or Dad to drive him to the swimming pool and wait for him. Yes, it will be a financial sacrifice to pay for the lessons. But the results will be worth the effort. Trevor will know how to swim![1]

There is a close analogy between this story and the spiritual training of our children. If our children have not received swimming lessons, we certainly don't toss them into the deep end of a swimming pool and expect them to swim. Likewise, we can't expect them to know how to face the challenges of living in a sinful world if they haven't received intentional spiritual training.

Throughout the progression from diapers to diplomas, one overarching issue confronts us as Christian parents: the spiritual growth of our children. What does it mean to "train a child in the way he should go"? Perhaps we have promised ourselves that we won't make the same mistakes our parents made with us, but beyond that we may be unclear about what is involved in spiritual training.

In the first session, you read in Deuteronomy 6:6-7: "These commandments that I give you today are to be upon your hearts. Impress them on your children. Talk about them when you sit at home and when you walk along the road, when you lie down and when you get up."

> *Spiritual training takes place one step at a time in the context of everyday life.*

But how do we do that? we wonder. *We've never done parenting before, nor attended seminary or taught a Bible class. And nobody modeled that for us very well (or at all).*

Fortunately, to train children to know, love, and serve

Jesus only requires the commitment to start the process of sharing spiritual truths with them—and do it intentionally. But the stakes are high. Many other booths in life's "carnival" are vying for our children's hearts and minds. They promise success, money, pleasure, fame, and many other things.

A CULTURE WAR

About 2,000 years ago, in the Roman governor's palace in Jerusalem, Pilate said to Jesus, "You are a king, then!"

Jesus answered, "You are right in saying I am a king. In fact, for this reason I was born, and for this I came into the world, to testify to the truth. Everyone on the side of truth listens to me."

Immediately Pilate replied, "What is truth?" and left the room. (See John 18:37-38.)

This question is still popular today. Many people in our culture demand that there be no absolute truth. "There are only situational ethics and standards," they proclaim. "If you think there are enduring standards, you must be a narrow-minded, uneducated, bigoted, archaic, right-wing weirdo!"

All around us, a culture war is taking shape. Should same-sex partners be allowed to marry? Is the Bible simply a book of mythic tales told by men? Aren't there many paths to God? Aren't Christ-consciousness, Krishna-consciousness, and Buddha-consciousness the same thing? Is Jesus the only way to heaven?

Noted speaker and nationally syndicated radio talk-show host Janet Parshall says, "If we are going to build a heritage of faith in our children, we must be intentional about instilling in our children the belief that truth is absolute. In your house, do your children know that the Lord is God and you are following Him? Mom and Dad, your babies do not live in a spiritual vacuum. Somebody's going to get there and occupy their hearts. The father of lies can't wait to slither up next to them and snatch them away.

"Paul wrote, 'See to it that no one takes you captive through hollow and deceptive philosophy, which depends on human tradition and the basic principles of this world rather than on Christ' (Colossians 2:8). Our children need to learn that God is in fact exactly who He said He is. They need to know that God is real. Otherwise, the first strong wind of the culture that blows on our children once they step outside our tent will knock them to the ground and take them captive to hollow philosophies."

We have to teach our children well because they live in a world that will take them captive if they don't know the absolute truth of the Bible. Satan is after every child. Society is becoming increasingly antagonistic toward Christians, the Bible, and Judeo-Christian values. That's why each of us needs to be intentional about giving our children spiritual training.

> **Studies reveal that as many as 70 percent of young people raised in church have not embraced the Christian faith as their own by the time they graduate from high school.**[2]

Our children need moral and ethical boundaries. They need lines of behavior that don't change based on opinion polls. They need godly character standards that will guide them away from sin and toward God's best. They need to develop a love for people who are headed for hell and need to be able to share the truth that sets people free. (See John 8:32.)

As we spiritually train our children, we are preparing them to know right from wrong and spend the rest of their lives growing in their relationship with the God who loves them and wants to be in personal relationship with them.

 Question

- In what ways are children today being exposed to "hollow and deceptive philosophy"?
- Why is it so important for our children to know that the Bible is God's absolute truth for today?

A 1994 Barna Research Group survey of 3,795 youth from 13 denominations revealed:
- Only 1 in 11 has a consistent, cohesive belief in absolute truth.
- By age 18, 27 percent of churched youth have experienced sexual intercourse.
- Forty percent think no one can prove which religion is absolutely true.
- Two in five say lying is sometimes necessary.
- Nearly 50 percent base their choices concerning moral matters on feelings and emotions.[3]

- How important is it for us to model for our children what it means to be a Christian in today's culture? Why?

ANY PARENT CAN DO IT!

Jim thought he was a great spiritual leader because he took his children to Sunday school every week. But one day three of his youngest children rebelled. "We don't want to go to church, Daddy," his daughter Janae said.

Surprised, Jim realized he had no idea what his children were being taught in church. "As I looked at my kids that day," he says, "I realized that I needed to assume the responsibility of teaching them biblical truth."[4]

But he didn't know where to begin or what to do.

For many of us, the notion of becoming intentional about spiritual training at home makes us tense, due to past failure or the fear of trying. If this is how you feel, it's okay. You can keep the training process easy and your priorities clear by remembering these four simple phrases:

Relationship Is Your Priority

Our children need more than knowledge of our faith; they need a relationship with our hearts! They need to know that we care as much about getting to know them as we care about praying over meals and getting to church on time.

If we want the values we teach them to stick, we must apply heavy amounts of the glue called love. We cannot have one without the other. Children perceive parental instruction through emotional lenses. Those lenses are framed by the quality of the parent-child relationship.[5]

True Stories from the Trenches

One evening we turned a trip to McDonald's into a faith lesson. We piled in the van and I handed a simple map that I had created to seven-year-old Kyle.

"Okay, Kyle. It's up to you to make sure we get to McDonald's." I started the car and proceeded down our street. At the corner, I stopped and looked over my shoulder at him. "Where do I go now?"

Kyle looked at his map. "You turn left."

"Naw," I told him. "I think I know what I'm doing; I don't think I need to turn left." I turned right instead.

Kyle burst out in frustration, "It says you're supposed to turn left."

At the next point of decision, I did the same thing. Soon Kyle was really mad.

When we ended up at a dead end, I said, "I guess I didn't know where I was going, did I?"

"That's right, Dad, because you were supposed to follow the directions," Kyle shouted.

"Well, now what are we going to do?" I asked.

"Go back to the beginning, and we'll follow the directions."

So that's what we did. We went back to the beginning. This time I followed the directions. During this second attempt at reaching McDonald's, we discussed what had occurred during our first trip.

"That's what happens when we don't obey the Bible," I told the children. "When we think we know what we're doing but don't follow the directions, we lose our way. God's Word is our direction for life."

An extra five minutes tacked on to an already planned trip became a powerful faith lesson.   —K. B.[6]

The Bible Is Your Handbook

God gave us an instruction manual for life—the Bible. It's full of what we and our children need to know and apply in daily life.

The Bible is "useful for teaching, rebuking, correcting and training in righteousness" (2 Timothy 3:16). In other words, it is relevant to all of us. It contains God's timeless truths, not merely religious ideas and ceremonies. We know that it is absolutely true.

Fortunately we don't have to know everything in the Bible before we begin teaching its truths to our children! What's important is that we start teaching them *today*.

If we believe that the Bible is God's Word, we will not only use it in teaching our children, we will demonstrate our belief by using it as a guide for our own lives!

Life Is Your Classroom

Where does a high school football player learn to play football? Most of the practical training takes place on a football field, right?

Where do our children learn foundational principles and concepts that will govern how they think, behave, and what their relationship with God is like? Moment by moment, day by day, during the hustle and bustle of everyday life.

> **We need to demonstrate to our children— through our own spiritual growth, by our example, and by when and what we teach—that our faith is about who we are, how we act, and what we do as well as about what we believe. When we teach our children about their faith in this way, connecting our teaching with our lives, our teaching method matches our message and becomes instantly more effective.[7]**

As important as memorizing verses or listening to a Sunday school teacher can be, no person becomes well established in the Christian faith by classroom instruction alone. As we've read in Deuteronomy 6:6-7, God has designed the world and us so that learning about the things of God and applying them in everyday life happen together.

Practice-what-you-preach parenting really works. Do we have to be perfect? No. It's what we do when we blow it that matters. Will we admit that we are imperfect? Will we admit we have shortcomings, ask forgiveness when appropriate, and keep asking God for help?

After all, every one of us—and every one of our children— is learning. Let's return to the swimming/teaching spiritual growth analogy. Even if we don't swim all of the strokes well, at least we are swimming in the water with our children instead of sitting on the beach observing from a distance.

Thought for the Day

We must earn the right to be listened to. As parents, we must realize that when we enjoy our kids today, we are earning the right to shape their values tomorrow. Children (and adults, too) are far more likely to embrace the values of someone they enjoy being with than those of someone they don't.[8]

Your Teaching Methods Should Target Your Child

The apostle Paul taught the Gospel message often, but he adapted it to fit the needs and viewpoints of various audiences. (See 1 Corinthians 9:20-22.) Likewise, this same principle applies to us when it comes to teaching our children.

What are the issues that are important to each child? What would it be like to walk in his or her shoes right now?

Perhaps one of your children or grandchildren likes to read stories. Another one likes to roughhouse in the family room. A third enjoys taking walks. Think of fun ways in which you can use each child's interests as a way to play with your child and teach truths about God and the Christian faith.

INTRODUCE YOUR CHILDREN TO JESUS!

When you take time to introduce your children to Jesus and He becomes their personal Lord and Savior, you are building an unshakable foundation for their lives. There is no more important work than being a Mom or a Dad.

The apostle Paul wrote, "By the grace God has given me, I laid a foundation as an expert builder, and someone else is building on it. But each one should be careful how he builds. For no one can lay any foundation other than the one already laid, which is Jesus Christ" (1 Corinthians 3:10-11).

> *Teaching spiritual truth to your children—teaching them to know, love, and serve Jesus—can be fun, exciting, and life-changing!*

Spiritual training doesn't happen by accident. It will happen because you decide to continue the process in your home today, building on what you did in Session One. And remember, if you don't provide intentional training, other people will.

MAKING OUR COMMITMENT STICK

Even after we parents know what we should do and agree to take action, we sometimes postpone the decision to start. If you are willing to start intentionally teaching your children or grandchildren spiritual truths, pray about your commitment. Ask God to help you begin this important training. Then read and sign the attached commitment card. This will demonstrate your personal commitment to spiritually train your children.

Commitment Card

On this _____ day of _____ 20 ___,

we are making a commitment before our God.

We, the family in this home, commit to fulfilling the task

of spiritual training. With God's help we will take up this

God-given task. We, the parent(s), will keep God's ways

on our heart(s) and "impress them on our child[ren].

We'll talk about them when we sit at home, when we

walk along the road, when we lie down and when

we get up" [per Deuteronomy 6:6-7].

Signed by our hands—held in the heart:

_____   _____

_____   _____

_____   _____

Just Try It!

Nature Walk (*no time limit, all ages*)
Materials needed: a Bible.

Take your children on a hike and explore the beauty of nature and the creativity of God the Creator.

Say: "We can't see God, but we can see evidence of Him in creation."

When you find a particularly pretty place, stop and read Psalm 148 together.

The Narrow Road (*20 minutes, preschoolers*)
Materials needed: toy blocks, a narrow board, two cinder blocks or other similar items, and a Bible.

Using items such as toy blocks, mark off a wide, eight-foot-long path across the floor in your meeting room or perhaps outside on a driveway if the weather is suitable. Make sure the path is clear and easy to traverse. Next to this path, set up two cinder blocks (or other blocks) about six feet apart and place an eight-foot 2x4 on them. (Make sure the 2x4 is centered on the blocks and secure so it won't easily fall off the blocks.)

Read aloud Matthew 7:13-14. Then say: "We're going to experience what it's like to walk the 'narrow path' in life and how it compares to the wide path. Then we'll talk about what that means for our lives."

Have family members take turns walking down the wide path. Then ask: "What was it like to walk this path?" [*Answers may include: It was easy; many of us could do this at the same time.*]

Next, have family members attempt to cross the "balance beam" or narrow path. Walk alongside children to be sure they don't fall and hurt themselves while crossing the board. (It may take a few tries for children to cross the narrow path. If they can't do it, hold them and help them walk without falling.)

Ask: "What was it like to cross the narrow path?" [Answers might include: It wasn't easy; I fell off; I needed help.] "How is trying to walk the narrow path like trying to obey?" [Answers might include: Sometimes it's not easy; sometimes we keep disobeying even though we know it's not right.]

Say: "When we face a choice, Jesus wants us to follow Him—to follow the narrow path. As we found out, that's not as easy as the wide path. But just as I was here to help you, we can have help to make it on the narrow path. We get that help from the Holy Spirit, who guides us; from church, which teaches us; and from Christian friends, who encourage us."[9]

☀ Good Grape . . . Bad Grape . . . Grape Juice? Mealtime Prayer/Discussion (14 minutes, late preschool to middle elementary school age)

Pray a mealtime prayer asking God to make you healthy inside and out. Then say: "In 1869 Dr. Thomas Welch successfully pasteurized Concord grape juice for his church to use in Communion. What color does your tongue turn when you drink grape juice? Which other foods make your mouth change colors?" (Give children time to respond.)

Say: "If you mixed together frozen grape juice and water, would it pour out as spoiled milk?" (Give children time to answer.)

Say: "Why not?" (Give children time to answer.)

Say: "What's on the inside comes out—whether it's good or bad. On the outside, Judas—a disciple of Jesus—looked like one of His followers, but on the inside he was very different."

Read Mark 14:43-46. Then say: "What seemed to rule in Judas' heart?" (Give children time to respond.)

Say: "Later, Judas realized that no amount of money was worth what he had done. How do you think he felt then?" (Give children time to answer.)

✸ Discussion Ideas

- "Name some thoughts and desires (good or bad) and tell which actions each of them will cause."
- "How can you get good desires and good thoughts inside you?"
- "Name five things you can buy with lots of money. How can they lead you away from Jesus?"
- "Which five things that don't cost money can lead you closer to Jesus?"[10]

Discussion Questions

The following questions are designed to stimulate discussion in a small-group setting such as a neighborhood Bible study, Sunday school class, or parenting class. We encourage you to listen to the audiotape for each session as a group before discussing the questions, but you may choose to only use this book if your group time is quite limited. It would be best if everyone in your group has the book and is excited about using it with their children.

Let's Talk About It
- In what specific ways is secular culture negatively influencing our children (radio, television, school, movies, peers)?
- What can we do, as parents, to combat our culture's sinful influences?
- Why do our children need more spiritual training than what they receive at church, even though that is very important?
- What do you think of when you read Proverbs 22:6? Why?
- What can we, as parents, do to keep up on what's happening in the culture? On what our children are being exposed to every day?
- If we are too busy to intentionally teach our children that absolute truth exists, what might the consequences be?
- Why is it so important for us to model what we teach our children?

The Legacy You Got, the Legacy You Can Give

No matter who we are, where we live, or what our goals may be, we all have one thing in common: a heritage—*the social, emotional, and spiritual legacy passed on from parent to child.* Every one of us is passed a heritage, lives out a heritage, and gives a heritage. It's not an option. Parents always pass to their children a spiritual, social, and emotional legacy— whether it is good, bad, or some of both.

LEGACY IS LIKE A THREE-STRAND CORD

Rev. J. Otis Ledbetter—pastor, teacher, and cofounder of Heritage Builders—compares these three components of legacy to a three-strand cord. Individually, each strand cannot hold much weight. But wrapped together, they are strong. God designed the social, emotional, and spiritual aspects of our legacy to be closely related, to be intertwined like a strong cord.

Luke 2:52 reads, "And Jesus grew in wisdom and stature, and in favor with God and men." Jesus, too, had a heritage. He grew in favor with God (*spiritual*), grew in favor with men (*social*), and grew in wisdom and stature (*emotional*), because everything that happens to us physically and mentally is registered in the emotions).

Today, if we don't pass along an intentional legacy to our children, our culture will gladly pass along its own legacy (as we read in Session Two). It's important to remember that passing on a spiritual, emotional, and social legacy is a process, not an event. As parents, we are responsible for the process. God is responsible for the product. We cannot do God's job, and He won't do ours.

THE EMOTIONAL LEGACY

In order to prosper, our children need an enduring sense of security and stability nurtured in an environment of safety and love. Jesus gave this wonderful, emotional invitation: "Come to me, all you who are weary and burdened, and I will give you rest" (Matthew 11:28). He understood, however, that we will get tired and face difficult challenges. Notice that He didn't say, "Come to me, and I'll rescue you from the pains of life." As parents, we need to create a place of rest for our children, not a place of rescue.

Sadly, many of us struggle to overcome a negative emotional legacy that hinders our ability to cope with the inevitable struggles of life. But imagine yourself giving warm family memories to your child. You can create an atmosphere that provides a child's fragile spirit with the nourishment and support needed for healthy emotional growth. It will require time and consistency to develop a sense of emotional wholeness, but the rewards are great! When an "emotional hit" comes, and it will, a child who is growing strong emotionally will be better able to cope with the pain than a child who has a weak emotional legacy.

To get an idea of the emotional legacy you received as a child, take a few minutes to complete the Emotional Legacy Evaluation on page 31. As you answer the questions, remember that a strong emotional legacy is pretty rare because emotions

Emotional Legacy Evaluation

Answer each question by circling the number that best reflects the
legacy you have received from your parents; then add your total score.

1. When you walked into your house, what was your feeling?
1-Dread   4-Stability
2-Tension   5-Calm
3-Chaos   6-Warmth

2. Which word best describes the tone of your home?
1-Hateful   4-Serious
2-Angry   5-Relaxed
3-Sad   6-Fun

3. What was the message of your family life?
1-You are worthless.   4-You are respected.
2-You are a burden.   5-You are important.
3-You are OK.   6-You are the greatest.

4. Which word best describes the "fragrance" of your home life?
1-Repulsive   4-Sterile
2-Rotten   5-Fresh
3-Unpleasant   6-Sweet

5. Which was most frequent in your home?
1-An intense fight   4-A strong disagreement
2-The silent treatment   5-A kind word
3-Detached apathy   6-An affectionate hug

Results:
Above 24 = Strong emotional legacy
19 – 24 = Healthy legacy
14 – 18 = Mixed legacy—good and bad elements
10 – 13 = Weak emotional legacy
Below 10 = Damaged emotional legacy

vary from person to person. Parents have to experiment to create an environment that fosters positive characteristics in their individual children because there is no "User's Manual" that applies to everyone.

As you ponder the legacy you received, be careful not to get locked into a negative critique of your parents. The point of this exercise is to understand more about the emotional legacy you received in order to be better prepared to plan the emotional legacy you give.

 Points to Ponder
A strong emotional legacy:
- Provides a safe environment in which deep emotional roots can grow.
- Fosters confidence through stability.
- Conveys a tone of trusting support.
- Nurtures a strong sense of positive identity.
- Creates a "resting place" for the soul.
- Demonstrates unconditional love.

Which characteristics would you like to build into the legacy you pass along to your children? Even if you don't hit the exact mark, setting up the right target is an important first step.

THE SOCIAL LEGACY

To really succeed in life, our children need to learn more than management techniques, accounting, reading, writing, and geometry. They need to learn the fine art of relating to people. If they learn how to relate well to others, they'll have an edge in the game of life.

In order to prosper, our children need to gain the insights and social skills necessary to cultivate healthy, stable relationships. As children mature, they must learn to relate to family members, teachers, peers, and friends. Eventually they must learn to relate to coworkers and many other types of people such as salespeople, bankers, mechanics, and bosses.

Nowhere can appropriate social interaction and relationships be demonstrated more effectively than in the home. At home you learned—and your children will learn—lessons about respect, courtesy, love, and involvement. Our modeling as parents plays a key role in passing on a strong social legacy. It is much easier for our children to cultivate healthy relationships if they see them properly modeled in the kitchen or family room!

Key building blocks of children's social legacy include:

- Respect, beginning with themselves and working out to other people.
- Responsibility, fostered by respect for themselves, that is cultivated by assigning children duties within the family, making them accountable for their actions, and giving them room to make wrong choices once in a while.
- Unconditional love and acceptance by their parents (or grandparents), combined with conditional acceptance when the parents discipline them for sinful behavior.
- The setting of social boundaries concerning how to relate to God, authority, peers, the environment, and siblings.
- Rules that are given within a loving relationship.

To help you understand the social legacy you received, take a few minutes to complete the Social Legacy Evaluation on page 34. The patterns we learned growing up tend to show up in present and future relationships. But as adults, we can change the patterns we adopted as children.

THE SPIRITUAL LEGACY

Parents who successfully pass along a spiritual legacy to their children model and reinforce the unseen realities of the Christian life. So, we must recognize that passing a spiritual legacy means more than encouraging our children to attend church, as important as that is. The church, of course, is to support parents in raising their children, but it is not responsible to raise children. Bible

Social Legacy Evaluation

Answer each question by circling the number that best reflects the legacy you have received from your parents; then add your total score.

1. Which words most closely resemble the social tone of your family?

1-Cruel and abusive
2-Cutting sarcasm
3-Chaotic and distant

4-Noncommunicative but stable
5-Secure with open communication
6-Loving and fun

2. What was the message of your home life with regard to relationships?

1-"Step on others to get your way."
2-"Hurt them if they hurt you."
3-"Demand your rights."

4-"Mind your own business."
5-"Treat others with respect."
6-"Put others before yourself."

3. How were rules set and enforced in your home?

1-Independent of relationship
2-In reaction to parental stress
3-Dictatorially

4-Inconsistently
5-Out of concern for my well-being
6-In the context of a loving relationship

4. Which word best characterizes the tone of communication in your home?

1-Shouting
2-Manipulation
3-Confusing

4-Clear
5-Constructive
6-Courteous

5. How did your family deal with wrong behavior?

1-Subtle reinforcement
2-Accepted in the name of love
3-Guilt trip

4-Severe punishment
5-Discussion
6-Loving, firm discipline

Results:
Above 24 = Strong social legacy
19 – 24 = Healthy legacy
14 – 18 = Mixed legacy—good and bad elements
10 – 13 = Weak social legacy
Below 10 = Damaged social legacy

From *Your Heritage*, © 1996, 1999 by J. Otis Ledbetter and Kurt Bruner. Published by Cook Communications. Used by permission.

Five Legacy Indicators

According to Kurt Bruner and J. Otis Ledbetter, five things you do are predictors of whether or not your children will receive the spiritual legacy you want them to receive. Do you:

1. Acknowledge and reinforce spiritual realities? Do your children know, for example, that Jesus loves everyone? That God is personal, loving, and will forgive us?
2. View God as a personal, caring being who is to be both loved and respected?
3. Make spiritual activities a routine part of life?
4. Clarify timeless truth—what's right, what's wrong?
5. Incorporate spiritual principles into everyday living?[1]

reading, too, is good. But unless we apply the Bible's truths and model them, even Bible reading will do little good.

Throughout the rest of this chapter, we'll explore aspects of spiritual legacy.

THE SPIRITUAL LEGACY YOU RECEIVED

When two people get married, each of them brings his or her individual spiritual legacy into the marriage. Sometimes this creates conflict. For example, what if one spouse grew up attending a mainline denominational church and participated in all kinds of church activities, but the other spouse became a Christian at age 20, attended various nondenominational churches, and never was active in any of them? Add the word perception to the mix, and things really get interesting. You see, the spiritual legacy each of us received is not just what your parents passed to you but how you perceived it!

Take a few minutes right now to complete the Spiritual Legacy Evaluation on page 36. Before you can chart a new, intentional spiritual legacy for your children and family, it's important to understand where you have been.

Spiritual Legacy Evaluation

Answer each question by circling the number that best reflects the legacy you have received from your parents; then add your total score.

1. To what degree were spiritual principles incorporated into daily
   family life?

   1-Never   4-Frequently
   2-Rarely   5-Almost always
   3-Sometimes   6-Consistently

2. Which word captures the tone of how you learned to view/relate to
   God?

   1-Absent   4-Casual
   2-Adversarial   5-Solemn
   3-Fearful   6-Intimate

3. How would you summarize your family's level of participation in
   spiritual activities?

   1-Nonexistent   4-Regimental
   2-Rare   5-Active
   3-Occasional   6-Enthusiastic

4. How were spiritual discussions applied in your home?

   1-They weren't   4-To teach
   2-To control   5-To influence
   3-To manipulate   6-To reinforce

5. What was the perspective in your home in regard to moral absolutes?

   1-If it feels good, do it!   4-Dogmatic legalism.
   2-There are no absolutes.   5-Moderate conservatism.
   3-Let your heart guide you.   6-Clear life boundaries.

Results:

Above 24 = Strong spiritual legacy

19 – 24 = Healthy legacy

14 – 18 = Mixed legacy—good and bad elements

10 – 13 = Weak spiritual legacy

Below 10 = Damaged spiritual legacy

From *Your Heritage*, © 1996, 1999 by J. Otis Ledbetter and Kurt Bruner. Published by Cook Communications. Used by permission.

Tip
Now that you have completed the three legacy evaluation sheets, fill out the Evaluate Your Heritage sheet on page 43. It will guide you in summarizing what you have discovered.

LOOKING AT THE LEGACY YOU WANT TO GIVE

Now that you have considered the legacy you were given, it's time to begin making intentional choices about the legacy you will pass to your children.

That means you have key choices to make. Which aspects of your legacy will you bring into your family? Which will you leave behind? How can you create a godly family legacy that will enable your family to prosper?

Here are a few practical tips:

Decide what you'll keep. Probably some things you received from your legacy are wonderful and need to be kept. Other things probably need to be thrown out. Perhaps you have a weak legacy that needs to be strengthened.

Whatever you received, you can now intentionally pass along the good. This isn't always easy. If you saw hypocrisy in your parents' lives, you may be tempted to throw out everything even though some of what you received was good. Don't. That would be like burning down the house to get rid of some bugs.

Realize that God can redeem even the "bad stuff" in your legacy. Sadly, most of us have at least part of our legacy that is weak or even awful. Maybe one of your parents was an abusive alcoholic. Maybe your mother didn't provide any nurturing. Maybe your father was a workaholic. Maybe you never knew one or both of your parents. Consider Abraham and his son, Isaac. Abraham lied to Pharaoh and told him that Sarah (his wife) was his sister (Genesis 12:10-19). Isaac, years later, did the same thing with his wife (Genesis 26:7-9).

Many parents today who received little in the way of a

positive spiritual, social, or emotional legacy in their childhood ask, "How do I give something I didn't receive? Nobody modeled this stuff for me." If you could say this too, remember that all is not lost. No matter what happened to you as a child, don't forget about Josiah, the Old Testament king. His father and grandfather were involved in many wicked things, including idol worship. But after eight-year-old Josiah became king of Judah, he reversed that trend. He sought God and purged Judah of idols and altars to false gods. He also repaired God's temple and started reading the Scriptures. (See 2 Chronicles 34.)

Like Josiah, you can choose which things in your legacy are no good and "throw them away." It's important to break the cycle of hurt by leaving the bad things behind and creating a new legacy. If that doesn't happen, statistics reveal that problem behavior continues to be passed on. Abusers tend to raise abusers. Liars tend to raise liars. Alcoholics tend to raise

True Stories from the Trenches

When I was six years old, my father died under tragic circumstances. Mom remarried a man who turned out to be an alcoholic.

For several years my family went through a period of turmoil that I could not understand since I was so young. Sometime after becoming a single mother the second time, Mom met Christ. It was then that the healing process in our family began, starting with my mother.

As a new, first-generation Christian, overwhelmed with emotional and spiritual grief, she was ill-prepared to spiritually train us. She was also only just beginning to become acquainted with God herself. Much of her malady was reflected in my siblings and me. However, as God began working in Mom's life, we kids observed how God enveloped her in love and gave her strength and the will to go on. Watching this changed us. We listened as she shared what she learned. We followed in her steps and found healing and spiritual growth for ourselves. Mom didn't need to be emotionally healthy to teach us; she just needed to follow God and lead us to Him. It was a journey we took as a family.   —Anonymous[2]

alcoholics. (Depending on what your situation was growing up, you might consider getting professional help from a Christian counselor or pastor.)

Unless we break the cycle, bad things will continue to be handed down from generation to generation. By God's grace we are able to break the cycle and pass along a different, positive legacy.

Chart a new course as you build a positive legacy for yourself and those you love. Research suggests that most fathers will parent the way they were parented. That means only a minority of fathers will change their parenting—even if their parenting is wrong!

Today, you can take positive steps to design a new heritage—the legacy you want to give and receive. Turn to the Designing Your Heritage sheet on page 40 and complete it.

Tip
When Dad spends time wrestling with the kids in the basement, he has done more to create a context for passing on the faith than when he reads them a Bible passage. Both are important, but the former makes the latter more meaningful.

When Mom plays a round of Go Fish with her six-year-old son, he learns to enjoy her as a person, not merely obey her as a parent. Again, both are important, but the former makes the latter easier to accept.

When the family takes a "backward" walk and everyone wears their clothes backwards, it builds relationships and shows that Mom and Dad are not always serious. They know how to have fun.

Everyone has the right to speak; we must earn the right to be listened to. As parents, we must realize that when we enjoy our kids today, we are earning the right to shape their values tomorrow. People are far more likely to embrace the values of someone they enjoy being with than those of someone they don't. So let's remember to have fun with our kids.[3]

Designing Your Heritage

This exercise is designed to help you identify the heritage you want to give. Drawing upon your responses to the previous evaluation sheets, write out the qualities you seek to give and receive.

First, identify the characteristics of the heritage you would like to give. Don't allow doubt or insecurity to hold you back. In the blank spaces below, list what you want your heritage to be, not what you think is realistic. (You may want to reverse the "bad" you received. For example: I want my children to have a relationship with God, not a religion.)

Then, next to the characteristics that you intend to give, circle the letter "K" for "keep," because they were solid aspects of the heritage you were given. Next to those that you consider weak in your own heritage, circle the letter "S" for "strengthen." Finally, next to those items in your heritage that you want to change in some way to improve, circle the letter "C" for "change." This step will become important later as you build your heritage plan, helping you zero in on those areas requiring the most intentional effort.

The Spiritual Legacy I want to give: Category

_____   K   S   C
_____   K   S   C
_____   K   S   C
_____   K   S   C
_____   K   S   C

The Emotional Legacy I want to give: Category

_____   K   S   C
_____   K   S   C
_____   K   S   C
_____   K   S   C
_____   K   S   C

The Social Legacy I want to give: Category

_____   K   S   C
_____   K   S   C
_____   K   S   C
_____   K   S   C
_____   K   S   C

SOME PLACES TO START

As you reflect on the family legacy you want to give, keep in mind the following principles.

Try different approaches. For years, many parents used just one or two methods to reach young hearts and minds with God's Word. The words "family devotions" still cause some otherwise courageous adults to flinch noticeably as they remember sitting bored and fidgety while Mom or Dad read from the Bible or a devotional book.

No doubt family devotional times were effective for many families, but times have changed. We can no longer assume that simply telling or reading our children something about God will have a positive impact. All of us are bombarded with words and images. How easily God's Word can be drowned out!

Customize your spiritual training plan. God made each of us unique, and our individual and personal relationship with Him is at the foundation of our Christian faith. He loves each of us individually and equally, and He knows us inside and out. After all, He designed and planned for every one of us long before our parents considered having us—and before we had our own children.

Just as every person is unique, there is no typical, effective way in which to pass your faith along to your children. You have a great opportunity to pass on your legacy to your children using ideas and approaches that work for your family! Not only can your "legacy choices" factor in your children's differences, your choices can build on these differences. You can have the joy of seeing your children grow in faith as they learn to apply God's principles to their particular situations.

WHAT IS YOUR FAMILY'S "HISTORY OF FAITH"?

Understanding your "history of faith" can make a huge difference in how you approach your children and intentionally build a legacy for your family. To help you see how to take advantage of your background, ask yourself which "generation" you are from as a Christian. Not surprisingly, how you answer will point out key areas of strength—and key areas of weakness.

The following Evaluate Your Heritage sheet will aid in this discovery, but here's a quick overview to get you started.

- A *"first-generation" Christian* has passion, enthusiasm, and no preconceived ideas concerning his or her newfound relationship with Christ. But challenges may remain, such as little knowledge about God and no heritage of godly faith.
- A *"second-generation" Christian* has some Bible knowledge, spiritual support, and experience with God but may question the faith, take God for granted, etc.
- A *"third-generation" Christian* can draw from a foundation of knowledge and generations of spiritual wisdom and maturity, but passion for the faith may be cold and there may be a tendency to do things the way they have always been done.

TAKE ADVANTAGE OF YOUR WINDOW OF OPPORTUNITY

It's no secret that young children up to age seven will believe almost anything you say. During the "imprint" stage of life, they easily absorb the fundamentals of your values into their young lives. This is the critical time in which to pass along your legacy, especially the spiritual aspect of legacy.

As children move through ages 8 to 11, they receive what parents tell them through increased ability to reason. If what we tell them makes sense, they grasp it. What we say and do makes an impression on them.

As children become teenagers, they move into what some have called the "game phase" of life. Parents become coaches, guiding and shaping. Having learned parental values, children go into life and test those values against real situations. If the values don't work, children find new coaches and try

Evaluate Your Heritage

1. Rate the general strength of each component of your heritage.

Spiritual Legacy:
Strong   Healthy   Mixed   Weak   Damaged

Emotional Legacy:
Strong   Healthy   Mixed   Weak   Damaged

Social Legacy
Strong   Healthy   Mixed   Weak   Damaged

2. List several characteristics that best summarize your leading legacy indicators. (Example: Spiritual Legacy—Religion emphasized over relationship.)

Good or Bad?

My Spiritual Legacy: _____

_____

_____

My Emotional Legacy: _____

_____

_____

My Social Legacy: _____

_____

_____

3. Finally, record any additional thoughts that could describe the heritage you were given. Which things do you appreciate about your home life? Which things cause the most pain? Which things have you taken for granted over the years? Which negative issues may be impacting your attitudes and behaviors today? Take a few minutes to contemplate these questions.

_____

_____

_____

_____

_____

out new things that might work. Sadly, we sometimes see our children making mistakes in the game of life and ignoring our offers of direction and guidance.

 Looking Back
How are you doing in your spiritual training plan?

Don't forget to keep in mind the four principles from Session Two:

- Relationship is your priority.
- The Bible is your handbook.
- Life is your classroom.
- Your teaching methods should target your child.

Just Try It!

✸ **Prayer** *(1 minute, all ages)*
Say a mealtime prayer, emphasizing what God has done for you and your family.

✸ **Constant Contact** *(15 minutes, ages 5 and up)*
Materials needed: a blindfold.

Activity: Using the furniture in your home, create a maze-like obstacle course. Then blindfold a child and have that one ask another child (or you) to guide him or her through the course by voice commands. When you or the other child stop giving directions, the blindfolded child should stop walking. (Pause every now and then.)

Do this again, if you have other children within the appropriate age range, until each person (including you) has gone through the course. To make it more difficult, change the course after each round, or change it after each person is blindfolded. That way no one can plan steps ahead of time.

Ask, after everyone has walked through the maze: "What made it easy or hard for you to go through the maze?" *[Answers may include: you gave me good directions, I listened carefully to what you said, etc.]*

Ask: "Can you think of how this game might relate to prayer?" *[Answers may include: we need to listen to God, God wants to give us directions in our lives, etc.]*

Share: "To get through this maze, you had to listen to the voice of someone who could see the maze. To get through the maze of life, or to understand what God wants you to do each day, you need to listen to what He is telling you. You need to communicate with Him constantly. The maze is like God's plan for your life. When you had your blindfold on, you couldn't see everything. But God sees everything ahead of you. If you stop talking to God and listening for His guidance, you won't know where to go next. You'll start to feel lost because you won't know what to do or where to turn. Prayer is a way to keep in constant contact with God."

Pray: Ask God right now to guide your family. If upcoming decisions must be made, pray for His clear direction in these decisions. Then take time to listen.

Wrap-up: Gather everyone in a circle and have each family member answer this question: "What's the one thing you've learned about God today?" Next, tell your children you have a new "Life Slogan" you'd like to share.

Today's Life Slogan: "Pray throughout the day to help you know God's way!" Ask each family member to repeat this slogan several times to help them learn it. Then encourage them to practice saying it during the week.

Close in Prayer: Allow time for each family member to share prayer concerns and answers to prayer. Then pray for each concern. Thank God for each family member, mentioning one special quality you appreciate in each person.[4]

✳ Not Hanging With the Crowd

Materials needed: carrot sticks for the appetizer; the main meal you are serving.

Pray: "Lord, I'd rather be like broccoli and stand up for You than be like chocolate and melt when the heat is on."

Say: "As we eat these carrot sticks, let's name some of the most unusual food combinations we can think of." *[Responses may include: chocolate pizza, cucumber ice tea, hamburgers with raisins on them.]*

Ask: "What do you think it would feel like to be the only kid at the school lunch table eating carrot sticks when everyone else is chomping fruity snack cakes? Why can it be hard being different?" *[Possible responses: feeling silly, wanting to eat what everybody else is eating, being embarrassed to stand out in the crowd.]*

Say: "Did you know that God calls us to be different from non-Christians? Moses, a Hebrew boy adopted by Pharaoh's daughter, could have lived in riches in an Egyptian palace. Hebrews 11:24-25 says," (read these verses to your children).

Ask: "What did Moses do instead of staying in the palace and doing what people expected him to do?" *[Possible response: Moses chose to stand out by refusing to be known as the Pharaoh's son and by choosing to be mistreated along with the people of God.]*

Read Exodus 4:18; 5:1.

Ask: "When God asked Moses to take the Hebrews out of Egypt, did Moses let his nervousness about being different stop him?" *[Possible response: No, he went to Pharaoh and told him what God had told him to say.]*

Read, then ask: "What does Hebrews 11:27 reveal about why Moses was able to do what he did?" *[Possible response: Moses did it because he saw "him who is invisible" — God. In faith, he did what God wanted him to do even though he stood out from the crowd.]*

Ask: "Thinking back to a situation when you needed to be different from other people at school or another place, how did you feel—and how did God help you?" *[Possible response: This will vary. Listen carefully to what each child says.]*

Ask: "What can be really good about being different? What three things that make you different can you be thankful for?" *[Possible responses: When I'm different because I'm doing what God wants me to do, God will help me. I'm thankful that I have freckles, that I love to read, and that I am the only one in the family who can _____ .]*

Discussion Questions

The following questions are designed to stimulate discussion in a small-group setting such as a neighborhood Bible study, Sunday school class, or parenting class. We encourage you to listen to the audiotape for each session as a group before discussing the questions, but you may choose to use only this book if your group time is quite limited. It would be best if everyone in your group has the book and is excited about using it with their children.

Let's Talk About It

- What have we already been doing, as parents or grandparents, to help our children receive:
    * a strong emotional legacy?
    * a strong social legacy?
    * a strong spiritual legacy?
- Why is it important for us to evaluate our own emotional, social, and spiritual legacy before we intentionally plan the legacy we want to pass on to our children?
- What are some of the obstacles that keep us from thinking about emotional legacy?
- What does a positive emotional legacy look like? How can we start building one in each of our children?
- Why is it important for us to use different, creative approaches with our children when giving a spiritual legacy?
- What surprised you—if you are willing to share—as you pondered the emotional, social, and spiritual legacy you received? Why?

What's Working?

This session discussed the importance of trying different approaches in order to reach your children's hearts and minds with God's Word. Which approaches are you using that seem to be working well? Which ones haven't worked well? Which new approaches might work? Feel free to brainstorm and come up with new ideas to try! Then compare notes the next time you get together.

Remember: You can't go wrong by trying new approaches. In fact, your efforts can pay great dividends later even though at the time it may seem as if a particular activity is a complete disaster.

King Josiah Did It!

Read 2 Chronicles 34 and answer the following questions:

    a. In what way(s) did Josiah reverse the bad legacy he received from his father and grandfather? (34:3-7)

    b. How do you think Josiah felt as he began smashing the idols in Judah? Why?

    c. What did Hilkiah the priest discover in the temple? (34:14-18)

    d. How did King Josiah respond when he heard what Shaphan read? (34:19-21)

    e. Because of the new legacy King Josiah intentionally created, what happened to the nation of Judah? (34:29-33)

    f. What may God be saying to us through this chapter about the opportunity we have to give our children a legacy different from what we received from our parents?

Creating Family Fragrance

When you hear the word fragrance, what comes to mind? A special perfume? Potpourri simmering in a kettle on a wood stove? The scent of pine trees during a walk in the mountains —or that odor you encounter on a fishing pier?

Did you know that every home has a family fragrance?

Some homes exude a caring fragrance of tranquility and cooperation. Family members and visitors in this type of home talk and laugh, share stories, and enjoy each other's company. A permanent light of love burns consistently, providing a glow of love, warmth, belonging, and beauty.

Sadly, other homes are full of tension and anger, unrest and criticism. Voices are harsh. Feelings are bottled up or vented loudly. Criticism is common. Confrontation is always ready to erupt. Domination and wounding replaces loving affection and affirmation.

CHOOSE YOUR FAMILY'S FRAGRANCE
Each child has a permanent memory bank. Even babies pick up what's happening in the home, recording impressions and

registering them through their senses into their imaginations. It is important, then, for us to create an atmosphere—a fragrance—at home to which our children will respond positively. We want to create a fragrance that inspires children to discover who they are and prepares them to face life's detours and chuckholes with a positive outlook.

What kind of fragrance would you like for your family? With a little effort, time, and creativity you can create an aroma that invites and inspires!

Can any of us create a perfect home environment? No. Nobody is perfect, and there are no perfect families. Disagreements will turn into squabbles, and at times the atmosphere will sour. But we can choose to improve the fragrance of our homes.

THE FIVE INGREDIENTS OF FAMILY FRAGRANCE

To help us remember how to create an inviting fragrance in our homes, let's look at the five ingredients of Family Fragrance using the acrostic AROMA.

Affection: Ingredient #1
Affection "is a consistent, loving act of the will, openly and sometimes spontaneously displayed toward its recipients."[1] It's the tangible sign of love. Affection is to be motivated by love and generated by an act of the will.

Jesus, who gave up His life on the Roman cross because of His love for us, asked us to love one another. So, our homes

True Stories from the Trenches

Donna, a single mom, creates an inviting atmosphere in her home despite her full-time job and long commute. Her secret? Every week, on her day off, one of her children takes a turn at requesting a favorite meal. That evening they all help in the kitchen—talking, cooking, and singing. Donna listens and answers questions, and everyone enjoys the food and pleasant family atmosphere.

should mirror that love. When love takes root in the hearts of family members, it consistently manifests itself in affection.

As parents, we can model the life of Christ by showing affection toward our children. Based on the model God gave us, our affection does not need a reason, only an object. We do, however, need a mature attitude and the will to show affection to our children simply because they belong to us.

Ways to Show Affection
There are many ways to share affection. Are hugs and kisses given away freely in your home? Sometimes just a simple hug or hand squeeze works wonders.

Guidelines for Cultivating the Fragrance of Affection

- Be sure your discipline of a child's bad behavior is not accompanied by withdrawal of your affection.
- Model intentional acts of affection—offering a glass of milk and a cookie, placing an arm around the shoulders, giving a compliment.
- Consistently model and teach an affectionate servant's heart. Helping your spouse and your children encourages unselfish attitudes.
- Freely say "I'm sorry" and "Please forgive me" at every appropriate opportunity, such as when you have judged a child incorrectly. If you are married, your children need to see you use these words freely with your spouse, too.
- Model and teach an attitude of affectionate communication in your home.
- Spend quantity time discussing with your children what's coming in their lives and guide them in ordering personal priorities.
- Provide the appropriate kind of affection to each child, remembering that the need for affection varies from child to child.

Jim Weidmann set up a "silent conversation" signal with his children. He will squeeze one of their hands four times, which stands for "Do you love me?" And they each will squeeze back three times, "Yes, I do." Then he will squeeze twice for "How much?" And they will squeeze back an answer.

Another way to show affection is to say, "I love you." At the end of a day, everyone in one family holds hands. All of them—mom, dad, brothers, sisters—talk about what happened that day or what'll happen tomorrow, then they pray about it. After the prayer, each family member tells all the other family members, "I love you." What a powerful affirmation!

Will you intentionally create a place where your children and friends can experience overwhelming affection? Children respond to parents (and grandparents) because, by an act of our will, we first love them and show affection.[2] Our affection also gives children the ability to love other people.

Thought for the Day

In moviemaking it may take two hours of shooting to get two minutes of quality film. It's the same with children. Quality time with your child results from quantity time.

Fragrance Tip for Waking Up Your Children

Here's a special way to wake them up in the morning, drawing on their senses:

Taste:	hot chocolate, orange juice
Smell:	scented candles, cinnamon tea, cocoa
Touch:	back, brow, and face rubs
Sight:	someone who treasures them as soon as they open their eyes
Sound:	your voice, talking with love; special music[3]

Respect: Ingredient #2

This ingredient of family fragrance involves "holding other people in honor so they may recognize their own true worth."[4] Showing respect for children helps them to develop manners and courtesy, inhibits self-destructive criticism, and leads to respect for peers, adults, and parents. Respect has to be taught. Children can't give respect if they have never received it. Unless we plant, practice, and nurture respect in our homes, we can't expect to harvest it.

Family fragrance is pleasant when family members honor each other's true worth. After all, each family member contributes a uniquely personal ingredient to the atmosphere of the home. If that value is doubted or stripped away, the entire family suffers. Independent and hurtful wills, sassy mouths, and self-righteous attitudes will rule.

Guidelines for Cultivating the Fragrance of Respect

- Use every opportunity to honor your child. Hang up those pictures or certificates of accomplishment!
- Either say something positive about other adults or say nothing at all.
- When your child becomes self-critical, ask questions to help him or her do a positive self-evaluation. ("How would you like this to be different? What can you do to help make it that way next time?")
- Respect each child's privacy, and give him or her a private place in your home (such as a bedroom). Don't invade it without permission.
- Avoid profanity in all conversations, and give a child using profanity proper instruction and admonition.
- Offer each child second chances. Second chances show that you have enough confidence in the child's character to trust that he or she will see a task or situation through to a positive resolution.[5]

Thought for the Day
Honor Your Family at Mealtimes

The best gift you can give to your family is your-self. Sit at the table as a family and be sure everyone joins in. Make mealtimes fun. Turn off the television and enjoy one another's company.

Order: Ingredient #3

Order—the opposite of chaos—also helps to create family fragrance. To help establish order in your family, follow and teach the "Three R's." No, not "reading, 'riting and 'rithmetic" but Rules, Roles and Rights.

Rules: Establish clear boundaries and ground rules for your household and consistently apply them.

Roles: Establish a sense of value in each family member by giving him or her a role to play in contributing to the family and household. Each person shares responsibility for maintaining cleanliness and a positive tone in the family.

Rights: As contributing members of a family, each person has the right to be heard. Involve children in important decisions; let them know they and their opinions are valued and taken seriously.

A house with no rules is a home in outward, visible chaos where children are allowed to make decisions they are incapable of thinking through and parents are at their children's beck and call. A home ruled by an iron fist, at the other end of the spectrum, is also a home in chaos, but covert, bubbling in fear and anger. So which parenting style works best? Usually a happy balance of creative freedom within generous boundaries conveys to our children—in deed, if not in word—how family matters are to be ordered. Seek moderation, an orderly rhythm in daily habits and rituals.

Be sure your child(ren) knows the rules of your home and the consequences of stepping outside of them. When the rules are honored and family members live according to them, an atmosphere of calm can prevail.

Guidelines for Cultivating the Fragrance of Order

- Make rules children can keep. As children see how order relieves outward chaos, they'll internalize and apply rules.
- Use planned family meetings to make decisions.
- Develop and follow your family's personal rhythm. Infants and young children need regular nap, bedtime, and daily schedules. Older children need regular reading and prayer time, family night activities, music or sport practice, and even dating time.

Merriment: Ingredient #4

Merriment, the fourth ingredient in family fragrance, is an easy one to grasp. It's "an atmosphere of enthusiasm coupled with uninhibited laughter and noise."[6] Home should be a fun place for everybody, including your children and their friends.

Enthusiasm and laughter make the other four ingredients of family fragrance stick together and keep a home lively and fresh. A lively household becomes infectious to all who live in it and come to visit. It's certainly not a boring, routine atmosphere.

What can parents do to make their homes a more fun place to be? All sorts of things! Some parents plan a fun thing to do every weekend—going swimming, taking a hike, building a kite, seeing a movie, or getting ice cream. Others guide their families into making up games, playing a unique version of baseball, or having family nights.

Of course, families sometimes face dark times when reasons for merriment seem far away. But Jesus came to bring us abundant life (see John 10:10, KJV)—joy in the midst of less-than-perfect circumstances. Sometimes we experience failure. Sometimes personal testings seem more than we can bear. Sometimes people hurt us. But we can still choose to focus on the positives.

The Cortez family created a fun way to deal with their typical "down" times. First, Dad repainted an old cookie jar with

True Stories from the Trenches

As their boys became teenagers, Lisa and Tom Rasmussen realized that jobs, practices, and after-school activities made it difficult to share dinner together. So they began getting up early and sharing a big breakfast with their sons. They also read Scripture, told stories, and discussed daily schedules. Years later the sons still get together at Mom and Dad's on Saturday mornings for breakfast![7]

cartoon characters and labeled it "Paper Cookies." Then family members wrote down 30 separate activities they enjoy doing together, gave each a number, folded them up to look like cookies, and mixed them into the jar. Whenever spirits were low, the family gathered around the jar, pulled out a paper cookie, and tried to do whatever was written on the paper.[8]

What can you do to bring more laughter to the dinner table? Or to create a pleasant evening with friends?

Every family faces times when nerves are raw, emotions are sensitive, and joking may be out of order. But often when a negative emotion enters the picture, things don't seem as bad if people take time to laugh.

Guidelines for Creating the Fragrance of Merriment

- Learn to laugh at yourself when things go wrong. This teaches children that it's okay not to take life too seriously. It shows them that you believe everyone will get another chance to try again.
- Laugh with someone who has seen the humor of a situation, not at someone who has yet to come to grips with the circumstances. Keep pointed sarcasm out of your home.
- Laughter and liveliness should have boundaries. Don't keep teasing someone when it's no longer funny. And don't poke fun at people in positions of authority over your children or those who are handicapped.

Add a Little Spice to a Meal Out

Go to a foreign restaurant and order meals that you and your children can't pronounce. If you go to a Chinese restaurant, don't allow your family to use anything but chopsticks—unless everybody gets so hungry that it's time to start using a fork again.

Affirmation: Ingredient #5

The last ingredient of family fragrance, affirmation, is a by-product of our realization that children flourish under the grace of positive reinforcement. J. Otis Ledbetter and his wife, for example, wrote a "Bill of Rights" for their children that says all children have a right to:

- Emotional stability. The key to this is unconditional love.
- Live in an affirming environment.
- Pursue their potential—finding and developing personal interests and natural talents.
- Make garden-variety mistakes—to learn problem solving, to fail, and to achieve success.
- Access the objective truth found in the Holy Bible.
- Have their own free time to think, play, imagine, etc.
- Receive nurturing and admonition.
- Grow in responsibility.
- Grow in knowledge.
- Be hugged.[9]

You need to be the head cheerleader for your child or grandchild, to be a dream maker and not a dream breaker. Children today receive lots of negative feedback from peers, friends, television, neighbors, and so on. Your children need to know that they are special. God created each of them!

One mother writes an encouraging note in her child's journal after the child has a bad day. Other ways to provide affirmation include saying "I love you," providing a loving touch on the shoulder or back, providing positive reinforcement, coming alongside when a mistake has been made, making sure positive feelings toward children are communicated, and eliminating all hurtful name-calling. Gail Ledbetter wrote:

> Our children need to know that there is nothing they can do to make God love them less, and there is nothing they can do to make God love them more. That knowledge alone can take a big load off a child. But they must also know that their parents feel the same way about them. That doesn't imply children should quit striving for excellence, nor does it give them license to do whatever they please. In this very negative world that has a bent toward knocking down the child or teen who tries to excel, parents need to be involved and ready to reassure a troubled child of God's unconditional love and their own abiding love for them.[10]

Another thing that must be affirmed in a child's life is where he or she will spend eternity. A plan on how to lead your child to Christ is included at the back of this book.

Just Try It!

☀ Table Talk or Car Chat *(ages 5–11)*
Try asking questions such as these during a trip, on the way to school, or at dinnertime: "How can we show affection without using words?" "What does Mom or Dad say or do for you that makes you feel loved?" Be sure to listen carefully to the answers.

☀ Create Special Memories *(all ages)*
Set aside an hour to tell stories about your past. In addition to being entertaining, stories connect children to their personal history. They can learn about your mistakes, who your favorite teachers were, and what you did in high school or college.[11]

☀ Getting to Know You *(all ages)*
Materials needed: Make one copy of the list below for each person at the dinner table; cook a family favorite entrée tonight.
Mealtime Prayer: Thank the Lord for your favorite food on the table. Then ask God to show you what's important to Him.
Appetizer: Ask your children to tell you how old you are, to list your favorite hobbies, and to reveal your eye color, without looking.
Family Discovery Night: Give each family member the following list. Then ask questions and try to guess each other's responses before the person being asked has time to answer.
• Coolest experience
• Bravest thing done
• Favorite holiday
• Favorite summer activity

- Special skill or talent
- Favorite food
- Least favorite food
- Favorite Bible story
- Favorite cartoon
- Favorite animal
- Favorite place to talk with God
- Favorite activity
- Favorite month
- Favorite thing to wear
- Favorite Bible verse

Table Talk (*Discussion questions you can ask*)
- How does listening to each other prove you care?
- Which action today showed your love to a family member?
- What did you learn about Jesus recently that you didn't know before?

Vitamins and Minerals: Read this verse: "Whoever has my commands and obeys them, he is the one who loves me. He who loves me will be loved by my Father, and I too will love him and show myself to him" (John 14:21).[12]

Discussion Questions

The following questions are designed to stimulate discussion in a small-group setting such as a neighborhood Bible study, Sunday school class, or parenting class. We encourage you to listen to the audiotape for each session as a group before discussing the questions, but you may choose to use only this book if your group time is quite limited. It would be best if everyone in your group has the book and is excited about using it with their children.

Let's Talk About It
- Why is family fragrance so important?
- What have we already been doing that promotes the following ingredients of family fragrance (AROMA)?
    1. Affection
    2. Respect
    3. Order
    4. Merriment
    5. Affirmation
- Why is it important for each of us to start thinking even more creatively about our family's atmosphere? What happens if we allow ourselves to get into a rut?
- Is it possible for us to dramatically change a household that doesn't have a godly family fragrance? Why or why not?
- How can we benefit from the experiences of others in this group as we try to intentionally create a pleasing fragrance in our homes?
- How might we parents and grandparents benefit from a fragrance of tranquility and cooperation in our homes?

What's Working?
• Which ingredients of family fragrance have some of us succeeded in creating (accidentally or intentionally)? What can
we do to help other people in this group improve the aroma
of the family fragrance in their homes?

The Influence of Traditions, Family Compass, and Teachable Moments

As parents, it is our responsibility to give our children a framework for living—to equip them with a strong sense of personal identity that comes from knowing who they are, who created them, and how they fit into the grand drama of life. In short, we want them to grow up knowing God.

Sadly, we live in an era in which nothing is considered sacred. Many people believe that God is dead, distant, or irrelevant and that subjective opinion is better than the Bible's objective truth in directing and explaining life's experience. But we can guide our kids to something much better—a personal relationship with the God who created them. We can help them obtain a sense of purpose and meaning. We can lead them to God's timeless truth and the profound hope that can be found only in Jesus Christ.

In this chapter, we'll look at key ways you can greatly help your children through Traditions, a Family Compass, and Teachable Moments.

TRADITIONS

For decades, the play *Fiddler on the Roof* has captivated audiences. The following words from this play emphasize another key element in the spiritual training plan—traditions.

> Here at Anatevka we have traditions for everything. How to sleep, how to eat, how to work, how to wear clothes. For instance, we always keep our heads covered and always wear little prayer shawls. This shows our constant devotion to God. You may ask, "How did this tradition get started?" I'll tell you. I don't know, but it's a tradition. And because of our traditions, everyone knows who he is and what God expects him to do.

Traditions play an important part in teaching our children the values they will need in order to navigate successfully through life. Teaching traditions is the "practice of handing down stories, beliefs, and customs from one generation to another in order to establish and reinforce a strong sense of identity."[1]

Instead of being dry, meaningless rituals, traditions can be fresh, fun, significant activities that help us to pass on a strong heritage to our children. The practice of traditions also helps build community by giving our children stability, dependability, and shared memories.

Traditions that link us to the past and connect us to the future force us to consider those people who have gone before us and those who will come after. Obviously not all traditions are good; in fact, some traditions may actually undermine a strong family heritage. But the Bible is full of God's admonitions to "remember" what He has done and has promised to do for His people. God knows that we need built-in reminders so we don't forget about the important things and people—including Him. Traditions help us remember.

As parents, we play a strategic role because we help to pass on the story of faith to our children. This is our responsibility and privilege. Unfortunately, in our passionate pursuit of individualism many of us have lost connection to our roots. We have forgotten that family traditions can connect us with who we are and what God expects us to do.

Through traditions you can create a strategic plan for passing on a spiritual growth heritage. Traditions create opportunities and events for us to be engaged with our children and walk with them through a path of spiritual growth. By creating traditions you can reinforce key values and pass along a spiritual legacy. It doesn't cost a lot to pass on valuable traditions, but you will need to invest time and thought and have the courage to move from ideas to action.

Set up milestones to be reminders and markers of your family's journey. Scripture records that many people built altars and "standing stone" memorials to God to honor what He had done for them. Joshua said, for example, "When your children ask you, 'What do these stones mean?' tell them that the flow of the Jordan was cut off before the ark of the covenant of the LORD." And, "These stones are to be a memorial to the people of Israel forever" (Joshua 4:6-7).

Milestones help us remember the important things. We prepare our children for the tests and challenges they will face by helping them observe and celebrate monuments of God's faithfulness. As parents, if we can discover God working in the ordinary and not-so-ordinary places, and can pass on this adventure to our children, we will have equipped our children with a heart for His kingdom.

Common milestones, which are a bit like "mile markers" in our children's lives, may include:

- Baby dedication—where parents affirm their dedication to raising the child to hear the gospel of Jesus Christ.
- Baptism of a child who accepts Jesus as Lord and Savior.
- Special weekend when a child is about 11 years old. Mother and daughter or father and son talk through the tape series, "Preparing for Adolescence", by Dr. James

Dobson (Ventura, Calif.: Regal, 2000). (Available from Focus on the Family: 1-800-A-Family.)

- Discussion of sexual purity based on "No Apologies" video when a child is about 13 (Vancouver, B.C.: Tyndale Family Entertainment/Focus on the Family, 1998). (Available from Focus on the Family: 1-800-A-Family.)
- Rite-of-passage ceremony when a child is about 15 in order to teach the disciplines of a godly man or godly woman. The child accepts the disciplines and responsibilities, parent moves from teacher to coach, and other people witness this special event and pledge support for the child, who receives a special family gift such as a cross.
- High school graduation—a time to explain the Christian worldview and hold a ceremony. Child receives the family signet ring (or other special gift).

Other opportunities to create meaningful traditions include:

- A blessing ceremony for each child to honor a special event or milestone in the child's life.[2]
- Special holiday celebrations. In order to show our children that they are important to God, we need to design kid-friendly family holiday traditions that are fun and significant. These may be as simple as reading the Christmas and Easter stories together and telling family stories, or may be as complex as providing volunteer services such as working at a soup kitchen on a holiday.

In Exodus 13:8 we read, "On that day tell your son, 'I do this because of what the LORD did for me when I came out of Egypt.'" A little bit later we read, "In the days to come, when your son asks you, 'What does this mean?' say to him, 'With a mighty hand the LORD brought us out of Egypt, out of the land of slavery'" (verse 14). We can help our children learn what the children of Israel needed to learn—that God is at work in our lives. Our goal is to maximize the holidays in order to teach our children spiritual truth by connecting the sights, activities, and smells of these special days with deeper spiritual truths. And we can do this by using ordinary holiday activities as training times.

Other suggestions include:

- Purchase a small nativity scene that is safe for little children to play with. The night you get it out, tell the Christmas story using the figures and animals.
- Buy a biblically-based pop-up book or storybook every year and read it during the holiday.
- Ask each child to write or draw three activities he or she would like to do during an approaching holiday season. Then have a family meeting and decide what you will do together.
- Have an evening of hot chocolate, popcorn, and watching a holiday-oriented video.
- Choose a Bible passage on thankfulness (Thanksgiving), Jesus' birth (Christmas), or Jesus' resurrection (Easter), and have each person read a few of the verses. (Young children can listen and draw pictures.)
- Have all family members write down or draw a picture on a piece of paper of why they are thankful for a particular holiday. Then put the poster on the refrigerator until the next holiday arrives.
- Before eating a special holiday meal, ask every person at the table to share two things about the person on his left for which he is thankful.
- Have a special holiday party, with finger foods, soda or sparkling juice in fancy cups. Give out individual achievement awards made from wide gold ribbon and silver stickers to each family member. (Reasons for the award might include: learned to read, met a new best friend, planted beautiful flowers, showed kindness to an elderly neighbor.)

Create Year-Round Traditions

Every day is special, so let's maximize our opportunities and make impressions that will last a lifetime. Will we open ourselves up to risk and failure? You bet. We must be courageous—willing to say no, to set boundaries, to be intentional about building family traditions, to parent differently than we were parented, to simply spend time with our children.

Year-round traditions might include:

- Annual camping trip.
- Summer canoe or bicycling trip.
- Sponsoring a neighborhood party once a year.
- Celebrate every child's birthday, and design elements that reinforce positive personal qualities of the birthday child.
- Devote each month of the year to a specific theme and do a special activity that relates to the theme. Also, read a Scripture passage that focuses on the theme. For example, March could emphasize friendship. Your family could bake cookies and deliver them with notes to special friends. You also could read Scripture passages dealing with friendship.

True Stories from the Trenches

When my younger daughter was in the fifth grade, some of the students formed "the club." It was quite an elite group, and the other children's worth was valued as to whether they were in "the club" or not. My daughter didn't seem affected by my reminder that they were being unkind and snobbish with their "club". God has His ways, however. One day my daughter came home devastated that she had been kicked out of "the club". At that point, God helped her to see how she had been treating others wrongfully.

—M.H. in Littleton, CO[3]

A FAMILY COMPASS

If you've ever been lost in the outdoors, you know the value of a good compass! It may be the only source of direction to lead you home. Similarly, our children need a Family Compass that provides a framework for living—a Christian worldview—that includes the beliefs and values necessary to navigate life's treacherous roads. A Family Compass provides crucial direction. It establishes a standard of normal, healthy living against which a person's actions, attitudes, and beliefs can be measured.

As parents or grandparents, we must take seriously our responsibility to equip our children with biblical beliefs and values. Take time right now to complete the Family Creed Worksheet at the end of the chapter, which will help you come up with a family creed you can follow. If you are married, set aside time to discuss and complete this worksheet with your spouse.

Four Compass Principles

Now let's briefly look at what Kurt and Olivia Bruner have called the four "Compass Principles" that govern and guide the process of giving an effective spiritual compass to the next generation. You can read about these in depth in their book *The Family Compass: Practical, Intentional Ways to Pass Godly Values on to Your Child.*[4]

Compass Principle #1: The Legacy Principle: What we do today will directly influence the multigenerational cycle of family traits, beliefs, and actions—for good or bad.

Verse to Remember

"Do not conform any longer to the pattern of this world, but be transformed by the renewing of your mind. Then you will be able to test and approve what God's will is—his good, pleasing and perfect will" (Romans 12:2).

You have already read about and discussed the importance of passing on a godly legacy in Session Three, so this will be a reminder.

The bad news is that there is no secret "six-easy-steps-to-perfect-children" formula. The good news is that with a little effort and a solid plan, you can give your children the ingredients for building a framework for life. Just as your parents passed on certain spiritual, emotional, and social patterns, you will do the same for each of your children. Truly, what you do today will directly influence the multigenerational cycle of family beliefs, traits, and actions. Even if you have been heavily influenced by negative generational cycles, you can break away from these bad patterns and launch a new era of good—for yourself and future generations.

The first and most important step in this process is to be sure that your own heart is right with God.

Compass Principle #2: *The Likelihood Principle: In the context of healthy relationships, children tend to embrace the values of their parents.*

In Proverbs 22:6 we read, "Train a child in the way he should go, and when he is old he will not turn from it." This passage, in effect, describes the Likelihood Principle.

Like us, our children are often drawn to accept the views of people they like and to reject the views of people they dislike. That's why we must focus on building strong relationships with our children. Teaching values in the context of an affirming and loving relationship is very effective.

Many children who are raised in Christian homes have rejected the values they were taught. Why? Often it is because their relationship with their mothers, fathers, or both parents was weak. So start today to build an affirming, loving relationship with your children.

Compass Principle #3: *The Lenses Principle: Our children need the corrective lenses of truth in order to navigate the deceptive roads of life.*

Just as neighborhood children scatter as soon as someone yells that a mean neighborhood dog is loose even if it's only a prank, we too live consistently with what we believe to be true even if our belief is false. The more our understanding of the world conforms to reality, however, the better our choices will be. Conversely, the more we operate under false assumptions the worse our judgment will be. To reach our objectives in life, each of us needs an accurate understanding of the world.

Our children enter this world with blurred vision—unable to discern reality. So we must intentionally help them sort through deception and learn to recognize truth. They need the corrective lenses of truth in order to navigate life. If we don't provide those corrective lenses, our children will follow wrong paths, develop unrealistic expectations, and make decisions that are not consistent with what God says is true. So we must help them understand and accept His truth—including His absolute moral truth!

Our children look at the world and interpret what they see through lenses that are heavily influenced by the culture around them. In our culture, distinguishing truth from lies can be difficult—especially when lies are presented as truth. Satan, the father of lies, uses lies in his battle for the hearts and minds of our children. Deception is powerful and influential. Our children need our intentional guidance to counter life's deceptions. Otherwise, they will accept an imperfect life map that provides a false view of reality.

Our culture preaches that all truth is relative, that each person decides for himself what is true. (A Barna poll revealed that nearly 70 percent of Americans believe there is no absolute truth.)[5] Instead of looking to God for understanding, it's easy for us (and our children) to look within and become our own source of truth. No matter how strongly we believe that our view of truth will work for us, if it is inconsistent with reality it isn't right! The same thing is true in our children's lives. Our children need to discover truth for themselves, but this is not the same as allowing them to create their own truth. We need to help them discover biblical truth.

We must help our children understand basic principles on which individuals and families can build a life of lasting purpose and meaning. God has given us His Word, and we can use it as a guide in teaching our children the truth of God by which everything can be measured. We can't take common reference points concerning truth, character, faith, morality, and other vital issues for granted. Our children need us to set standards based on God's rules and to instill values based on God's perspective.

As we've seen in earlier sessions, just because we parents or grandparents are Christians doesn't mean that our children will grow up to be Christians. We must intentionally pass on to our children the spiritual truths God has given us in His Word. What happened to Eli, an Old Testament priest, is a sobering reminder of why a Family Compass is so important. While he conducted his priestly duties by the temple of God, his sons were committing great sins. Finally Eli rebuked his sons, but they didn't listen to him. So God punished Eli and allowed his sons to die.

Start today to develop a Family Compass that will give your children the direction and biblical worldview they need!

Compass Principle #4: The Learning Principle: Our children can only learn what we teach them in a manner that will reach them.

In order to teach our children, we need to know two things about them.

1. Their basic nature. The Scriptures reveal that our children are made in God's image (Genesis 1:27). As such, they have:

- God's mental likeness—able to reason and exercise their will. We can hold them accountable for their choices, teaching them to counter their natural, sinful impulses.
- God's moral likeness—a conscience and the ability to distinguish right from wrong. We must help them

develop and maintain an informed, sensitive conscience by distinguishing truth from error and right from wrong.

• God's social likeness—the ability to love and relate to other people. Because children by nature will resist authority, we should expect resistance to our instruction and find ways to push past surface rebellion in order to tap their deeper yearnings.

Our children possess wonderful, awe-inspiring qualities. Unfortunately, as part of the human family, our children also were born with a fallen, sinful nature that is prone to evil.

2. Their stage of life. The better we understand our children, the better equipped we will be to teach them in a way that will reach them. When we understand three key stages of child development, we can create an intentional plan for teaching them and can learn to create and capture opportunities to impress our Christian beliefs and values on their hearts.

Ages 7 and under: During this Imprint period, children are all ears, eager to accept our values and beliefs without much question. Games, stories, songs, and memorization can be powerful tools in teaching Christian beliefs and values.

Ages 8 to 14: During this Impression period, children are open to our direction and influence, asking questions to learn why. But they don't accept blindly. Now it's time to teach the rationale behind our beliefs, using logic, so they learn to think for themselves.

Ages 15 and up: During this Coaching period, we need to equip our children to make their own choices in an informed, mature manner. We can help them learn to articulate what they believe, challenge their thinking, and remind them of the basics, but we must not treat them as we did when they were younger. Pat answers won't cut it. We must wrestle with tough issues along with them in an honest, authentic manner. We may not have all the answers, but we can give them direction.

TEACHABLE MOMENTS

Creating special, teachable moments with your children is one of your most precious, and sometimes most difficult, responsibilities! You can plan special activities that give you opportunities to have fun with your family and also teach important truths. What are some of these activities?

- Go see a movie and discuss it afterward at a favorite restaurant.
- Walk in a park and talk about God's creation.
- Attend Christian events like concerts and youth rallies.
- Ride bikes, hike, or go fishing and teach simple spiritual lessons in the midst of the fun.
- Play a game together.
- Read a book together.
- Go go-carting and talk about "winning the race of life" with God's help.
- Make tunnels with blankets, card tables, chairs, boxes, and whatever else you have. Then read Psalm 91, eat popcorn, and talk about how God covers us with His love.
- Select one of the many ideas from the *Family Nights* books in the Heritage Builders series suggested at the end of this book.

You can also capture teachable moments throughout the day and turn them into spiritual moments when you can teach and impress biblical values, beliefs, and principles on your child. Capturing teachable moments is one of the easiest methods to use in spiritual training. It's as simple as paying attention to the world around you and presenting it to your child from a godly viewpoint. After all, the best learning takes place in the context of real life, and many events in life are ready-made opportunities to teach and train your child. The key lies in recognizing the moment when truth and life collide.

What kinds of moments can you capture?

- Make the most of everyday opportunities to teach by example. (Children see how you handle money, temptation, frustration, windfalls, etc.)
- When your child asks questions or is dealing with life and its problems, take time to provide a thoughtful answer.
- When you give your child a bath, pray with him or her and talk about the story of Moses floating in the little basket.
- As you drive to the store or head to an athletic contest, redeem some of the time in the car by using it to intentionally teach spiritual truth. It's a chance to bring up a topic you want to discuss, let a child talk about what's on her mind, or listen to a Christian tape or CD.
- As son or daughter shares a difficult situation he or she is going through, listen carefully. If you have felt or experienced something very similar, you might share what happened or how you felt.
- At mealtime, pray about an important decision your child must make. Or take a moment to comment on how God is working in your life. Keep the discussion short, unless things become really lively. Make your topics fit what happened that day.
- Do a chore with your child, and while you work, share something God has been teaching you.

Remember, what's important is for us to live out our spiritual principles with our children. The day-to-day activities really make a difference. We all can find ways to create and capture opportunities to connect with our children!

Ways to create opportunities:

- Read your child a Bible story at bedtime instead of a fictional story. Bedtime is also a great time to start teaching children to develop the habit of a daily time with

Four Keys to "Teachable Moment" Success

1. Keep a teachable moment short and simple. It's best to let the moment speak for itself.
2. Be proactive. If you find teachable moments only when a kid makes a mistake, you are preaching instead of coaching. Find positive lessons that affirm your child and your relationship with him or her. When you need to correct, offer correction constructively and in love.
3. Remember you are not alone. God is your child's heavenly Father, and He wants to help in the parenting process. When you decide to partner with Him in raising your child and ask for His help and wisdom, He will be right there with His grace. Ask Him to help you recognize teachable moments and respond appropriately.
4. Use a balanced approach in love and grace. If you received little consistent training in the Christian faith when growing up, you may tend to overemphasize instruction. If you received too much instruction, you may focus too much on being a nurturer and not enough on being a teacher and trainer.

God. As you read the Bible and pray with your child, you can emphasize getting to know God and help the child develop a relationship with Him.

• Say a prayer at dinner that relates to what your child has experienced during the day.

• Rent or buy some "Adventures in Odyssey" dramatized audiotapes or videotapes. Published by Focus on the Family, these stories take kids ages eight and up through many exciting adventures and teach important lessons about the Bible, God, and the Christian faith. After you have finished an adventure, discuss the main teaching points and personalize the lesson to suit your children's lives.

• Create meaningful opportunities for spiritual training by setting aside regular, fun "Family Nights" that bring the family together. Heritage Builders offers a number of "Family Nights" idea books that are full of easy and fun activities.

Tips for having effective Family Nights include: having fun, keeping lessons simple, encouraging participation, going with the flow, staying out of ruts, and doing Family Nights once a week (if possible).

• Share a story about what God did in your life years ago. These "snapshots" of God's involvement in your life are a great way to connect your children's faith to reality.

True Stories from the Trenches

Jim Weidmann noticed that his children were constantly getting on each other's case, saying things that were not nice to each other. So Jim promised to teach them a lesson during the next "Family Night" because their conversation wasn't honoring God.

One at a time, Jim brought each of his children from a separate location and had them stand in front of him. Then he asked his oldest son, who was blindfolded, "What is the most powerful weapon in the world?"

His son replied, "A gun or a bomb."

Jim then placed a long, soap-covered cow's tongue (from the grocery store) in his son's hands.

"Yuk! What's this?" his son asked.

"You are holding the most powerful weapon in the world," Jim replied. "I know this to be true because James tells us that you need the power of God to control this thing." Then Jim removed the blindfold.

His son has never forgotten this illustration.

- Celebrate annual occasions in which you can inject spiritual meaning, such as remembering the day a child became a Christian.

One final hint: Sometimes kids just want to relax, have fun, and goof off. Be sensitive to their needs and wants. Sometimes rather than trying to squeeze in one more truth, talk from your heart or just listen. At times, give your children a choice of what they'd like to do. Maybe they'd rather sing Bible songs than talk.

Thought for the Day

We are part of His story. We are privileged to maintain the continuity of the message—the message of grace. God, in His grace, has given us children, and given us eternal life. It is our role to connect our children with God's grace. It is our responsibility to not only prepare our children for life, but to prepare them for eternity.[6]

Family Creed Worksheet

A sample family creed: Our family exists to help each member grow to his or her full God-given potential. We believe that we can enjoy a life of meaning and fun, and we seek to pass the abundant life on to others.

Begin to develop a family creed for your family. Use the following worksheet.

1. What is important to you?

2. What is important to God? (List Scripture verses.)

3. What gifts and talents has God given our family members?

4. How can these be used to contribute to others?

5. What is our family's potential? With God's help, what could we do to serve Him?

6. What are some key strengths from our family history?

7. What are some key weaknesses from our family history?

8. How can we use our strengths and weaknesses to benefit us now and in the future?

9. What steps can we take to pass on a godly and healthy heritage?

10. What have we done to strengthen our connection with God's family? What could we do?

11. What seems to be working to help us grow spiritually strong?

12. What Scripture has a special history for our family? How have we seen God's Word become a reality in our family life?

13. How has God's Spirit empowered our family? How have we seen God's power in our family?

Just Try It!

❋ Prayer *(1 minute, all ages)*

Say a mealtime prayer, thanking God for giving us the Bible so that we can know truth that doesn't change. Also, thank God for giving us time to do special things [*such as* _____] as a family.

❋ Parent Report Card

Ask your children to spend a few minutes grading you on how well you are doing as a mother, father, grandmother, or grandfather.

Description	Grade
1. Shows he/she loves me	_____
2. Is interested in my feelings	_____
3. Spends enough time with me	_____
4. Listens to what I say	_____
5. Trusts me	_____
6. Enjoys being with me	_____
7. Is truthful	_____
8. Makes family a priority	_____
9. Makes fair decisions	_____
10. Disciplines me when I deserve it	_____
11. Admits when he/she is wrong	_____
12. Controls his/her anger and words	_____

Follow-up discussion questions to ask each child separately:

- What's the best part of my relationship with you? Why?
- Which part of our relationship do you think needs the most improvement? Why?

- If I could change anything in order to be a better parent, what would you like me to change? Why?
- What do you think you might change in order to make our relationship better? Why?
- If you could have me start today to do one or two things for you, what would they be?[7]

✹ Run for Your Life

Say: "In the book *The Tale of Peter Rabbit*, Peter the rabbit disobeyed his mother—big time—by going into Mr. McGregor's garden! Naughty Peter was tempted by all the goodies in the garden and hopped where he wasn't supposed to hop. Then Mr. McGregor, the gardener, went after Peter, who narrowly escaped becoming Mr. McGregor's supper. Just glad to be alive and back in his own home, Peter accepted his dose of discipline and went to bed early."

Ask:

- "If you had been Peter, which lesson might you have learned from nearly being caught in the garden?"
- "How well do you follow directions?"
- "Peter's downfall—his temptation—was the garden. Which 'garden' in your life tempts you to disobey?"
- "Why is it so important for you to follow directions?"
- "What can happen to you if you don't follow directions?"

Read: "Children, obey your parents in the Lord, for this is right. 'Honor your father and mother'—which is the first commandment with a promise—'that it may go well with you and that you may enjoy long life on the earth'" (Ephesians 6:1–3).

Say: "Imagine that your backyard, or a field or park close to your home, is full of things that tempt you to disobey. They are coming to life and are out to get you. But you need to cross through that place safely. What do you need to help you?" [*Possible responses may include: a shovel to bury the bad things, determination, a cell phone to call for help, God's help to avoid the temptations, the help of a parent or grandparent.*][8]

✸ The Most Important Commandment
Materials needed: a Bible.

Ask: "If you had to pick the most important commandment or instruction in the Bible, what would you say it is?" *(Note: Listen to your child's suggestions, affirming their importance.)*

Say: "All the instructions in the Bible are important. But somebody asked Jesus that same question. Let's read about it."

Read Mark 12:28–31.

Ask: "Which part of Jesus' answer do you think is the most important commandment?" *(Note: Help your child identify loving God as most important.)* "How do you show God that you love Him?" *(Listen carefully to the child's answers.)*

Pray: "Dear God, Thank You that _____ [child's name] shows [his/her] love for You by _____ [name the ways your child identified as showing love.] Thank You that You love _____ [child's name] very, very much! And help _____ [child's name] to know how much I love [him/her], too. Amen."[9]

Discussion Questions

The following questions are designed to stimulate discussion in a small-group setting such as a neighborhood Bible study, Sunday school class, or parenting class. We encourage you to listen to the audiotape for each session as a group before discussing the questions, but you may choose to use only this book if your group time is quite limited. It would be best if everyone in your group has the book and is excited about using it with their children.

Let's Talk About It
- Why do our children need a "Family Compass"?
- How has our culture's view of truth changed since we were children?
- How did you feel as you completed the "Family Creed Worksheet" at the end of the chapter? Why?
- Why is it so important for us to have our hearts right with God before we make plans to influence the legacy we give our children?
- How can we teach our children about the difference between biblical truth and subjective opinion?
- Why is it so important for us to understand which stage of life (Imprint period, Impression period, Coaching period) each of our children is in? How might we as parents and grandparents use this understanding in practical ways?
- What's the difference between creating a teachable moment and capturing a teachable moment?
- What did you think about the "traditions" part of this chapter? Why?
- Which traditions would you like to establish in your family for everyone's benefit? Why?

Looking Back
Which ingredients of Family Fragrance have
some of us succeeded in creating since our last
session together? What "AROMA" ideas would you like to
share so that all of us can improve the Family Fragrance in
our homes?

Tailoring Your Spiritual Growth Plan to Your Unique Family

Recognize Your Successes . . . and Try Some New Things, Too

Whether you are new at intentionally teaching your children through a spiritual growth plan or have been doing it for years, recognize your successes. Perhaps you pray with your children at mealtimes or at bedtime. Or you take your children to church regularly. Or you try to do fun activities as a family at least once a week and share truth about God during appropriate moments. The key is to appreciate what you have already done and start trying some new things today!

If you feel a bit insecure about trying something new or adding more responsibilities to your already busy life, that's okay. Many other parents and grandparents have been in your shoes. Maybe you tried various approaches in the past and became discouraged. Maybe you've tried a few activities, seen them succeed with your children, and are excited about doing more.

Parents (and grandparents) around the world are effectively using the principles in this book with their children.

These parents are by no means "super parents." They come from all different socioeconomic, cultural, and family backgrounds. But they recognize how important it is to teach their children truths about God and their relationship with Him.

As you put what you've read here into practice and perhaps use other Heritage Builders books (see the recommended resources at the back of the book), take Deuteronomy 6:6-7 to heart and ask God to use your efforts to bless your children:

> These commandments that I give you today are to be
> upon your hearts. Impress them on your children.
> Talk about them when you sit at home and when
> you walk along the road, when you lie down and
> when you get up" (Deuteronomy 6:6–7).

DEVELOP YOUR OWN SPIRITUAL HERITAGE PLAN

Now think about the spiritual heritage plan you will be putting into action. Use the following chart to decide what you plan to begin doing with your children—or what you will add to your ongoing plan.[1]

May God bless, encourage, and strengthen you as you seek to better know and love Him. May He also use your spiritual growth plan to guide your children into a personal relationship with Him that will make a life-changing, eternal difference.

ADJUSTING TO YOUR FAMILY'S UNIQUE PERSONAL STRENGTHS

It's no secret that each child has a unique identity and personality. Even identical twins can be quite different! So it's important for us to identify the traits with which we—and our children—are equipped. By recognizing our children's differences, we can better tailor effective spiritual training to their needs and interests.

Right now, look at the Child's Personality Survey on page 91.

Spiritual Heritage Plan

PRAY DAILY

Currently:	*Sample Plan:*	*Your Plan*
• Pray together at mealtime. • Pray with children at bedtime.	• Provide daily prayer covering for family; if married, pray together for family at end of day.	

WEEKLY FAMILY ACTIVITIES

Currently:	*Sample Plan:*	*Your Plan*
• Watch a favorite television show and play a board game together.	• Choose one night a week to hold a "Family Night" activity.	

CAPTURE THE MOMENT

Currently:	*Sample Plan:*	*Your Plan*
• Read a bedtime story.	• Read devotional stories at dinner. • Let children listen to *Adventures in Odyssey* tapes from Focus on the Family after bedtime prayers.	

ATTEND CHURCH ACTIVITIES

Currently:	*Sample Plan:*	*Your Plan*
• Attend church weekly as a family.	• Get children involved in Sunday school and/or youth group(s).	

This survey is designed for younger children, who can complete it themselves or have their parents/grandparents fill it out for them. (Note: as soon as the survey sheet is completed for each younger child, move to the next section, Explanation of the Surveys.)

The Personal Strengths Survey, a related survey designed to help parents, grandparents, and older children learn more about their unique personal strengths, can be found on the Heritage Builders Web site. Take a few minutes to look it up. If you don't have access to a computer, skip this part for now and ask a friend to download copies of the Personal Strengths Survey—one for each parent/grandparent and one for each older child in your immediate family. As soon as possible, each of you should complete the survey, being sure not to take longer than three minutes to fill it out.

Explanation of the Surveys

Focus on the Family's Parents' Guide to the Spiritual Growth of Children explains the four personality types explored in the Child's Personality Survey. These personality types are symbolized by

True Stories from the Trenches

It was another busy day for Anna. She hustled her three children into the van for a 25-minute drive across town to soccer practice and a baseball game. The kids were noisy and fidgety; Anna had a headache.

"Hey, Mom," the nine-year-old yelled, "can we listen to Adventures in Odyssey?"

"Nathan, you can't hear anything when you're this noisy," Anna replied.

Immediately the kids agreed to be quiet, so in went the cassette tape. Later, on the way to the baseball game, Anna discussed the show's lesson with her oldest, the 11-year-old. What could have been an awful time in the car became a peaceful time when the children had fun and learned important biblical truths.[2]

Child's Personality Survey

Name _____

*For your younger children, read the following descriptions aloud.
Circle or put the child's initial by each description
that is a consistent character trait.*

L	B
• Is daring and unafraid in new situations	• Is neat and tidy and notices little details
• Likes to be a leader; often tells others how to do things	• Sticks with something until it's done; doesn't like to quit in the middle of a game
• Ready to take on any kind of challenge	• Asks lots of questions
• Is firm and serious about what is expected	• Likes things done the same way
• Makes decisions quickly	• Tells things just the way they are
Total relevant statements = _____	**Total relevant statements = _____**

O	G
• Talks a lot and tells wild stories	• Always loyal and faithful to friends
• Likes to do all kinds of fun things	• Listens carefully to others
• Enjoys being in groups; likes to perform	• Likes to help others; feels sad when others are hurt
• Full of energy and always eager to play	• Is a peacemaker; doesn't like it when others argue
• Always happy and sees the good part of everything	• Patient and willing to wait for something
Total relevant statements = _____	**Total relevant statements = _____**

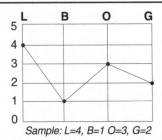

Sample: L=4, B=1 O=3, G=2

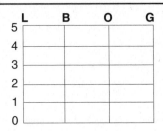

Adapted from *The Two Trails,* © 1998 by John Trent and Judy Love (Nashville: Tommy Nelson, 1998).

four animals: lion, beaver, otter, and golden retriever. As you read the descriptions for each animal below, determine which one matches each child most closely

Lions (High "L" People)

"Lions" are assertive, take-charge people who like leading and being in charge. You rarely have to motivate them—just point them in the right direction. They are decisive and will strive to accomplish what others say is impossible. When a Lion's strengths are balanced with loving sensitivity, he or she will be a wonderful leader, friend, and parent. But Lions can also become too assertive and insensitive in word and action, communicating that a project is more important than the people involved.

How to Approach Lions
- Emphasize God's purpose for them and the world.
- Let them have a say in how things are done and help develop the program; they'll be committed to it.
- Use Bible stories about leaders such as David and Moses.
- Explain God's "Big Story," from Adam and Eve to Jesus' death, resurrection, and eventual return.
- Give their faith a purpose. To be motivated, Lions need to understand the goal. Allow them to lead, help, and teach others—including siblings.

Otters (High "O" People)

"Otters" love to have fun. They love life, and especially people. They are great networkers. Maybe they don't know everybody's names, but everyone is their best friend. Usually Otters are not into details. They often complete term papers the night before they are due, put off doing routine tasks, and tend to be late. They often start projects but have a hard time completing them. If Otters are given responsibility and an understanding of how their lateness affects other people, however, their sensitivity can be a tremendous asset, especially when they become spiritual leaders in the home or ministry.

How to Approach Otters

- Emphasize their relationship with other people and God; life to them is all about people.
- Emphasize fun, and vary spiritual training. Routines cause them to lose interest.
- Use Bible stories about people such as Peter, Esther, and King Joash.
- Explain God's desire for relationship, His deep love for people, and His desire to save everyone.
- Guide them into a good social structure and make their faith fun.

Golden Retrievers (High "G" People)

These people are sensitive and caring and have a hard time saying no. Golden Retrievers are compassionate and wonderful team players. They care about the individual and want to include everybody. They go with the flow, adapting as needed. They watch other people make mistakes and avoid making the same ones, thus avoiding pain.

Golden Retrievers make people around them feel loved and accepted, but due to their sensitivity their feelings are easily hurt. If your child is a Golden Retriever, remember that he or she soaks up friction like a sponge. Even a young Golden Retriever will try to solve parents' problems or take on emotional burdens far beyond his or her years.

How to Approach Golden Retrievers

- Emphasize God's personal care and love for them—and the world. Individual care, acceptance, and love are the keys to their hearts.
- Emphasize your relationship with them. Do things with them and they'll feel safe and take part eagerly. They require the context of personal relationships.
- Use Bible stories about people taking care of people and how Paul traveled to help people know Jesus.

- Explain John 3:16, emphasizing that God loved and gave. Commitment and love are important to Golden Retrievers.
- Help Golden Retrievers establish right friendships and pray and care for other people. Make their faith a caring faith.

Beavers (High "B" People)

"Beaver" personality types are detailed and organized. A Beaver remembers, for example, to bring what he or she promised to bring to a social gathering. They mentally file things away—even what somebody said years ago—so they can always find them.

Beavers both start and complete a few projects a year. They are predictable, they follow through, and they make lasting contributions. They analyze things well and take things apart successfully.

If pushed to an extreme, Beavers can be harsh critics of other people—and themselves—if goals are not met.

How to Approach Beavers

- Emphasize truth and right (as opposed to wrong).
- Be consistent and predictable with Beavers. They gain safety and security when they know what's coming and when it's coming.
- Use Bible stories that emphasize principles and right and wrong ways of doing things (Adam and Eve, for example, or the Pharisee and the tax collector).
- Explain the details of salvation. Beavers want to know that God's truth is based on solid fact.
- Find specific answers to their questions so their faith makes sense. Beavers need reasons and "proofs" for doctrines and beliefs.

Once we identify our children's strengths (and our own), we can use what we learn to praise our children and appreciate their unique personalities. As we develop our family's spiritual growth plan, we should try to match our children's unique strengths to things that our children enjoy. Lions, for example, like options from which to choose. Otters like fun family training time, such as playing a board game with other people. Beavers like to go from point A to point Z systematically. A young Golden Retriever would like to hear a story read to him or her.

If your family is a wild combination of these four animal types, you'll face obvious challenges—especially since your own personality strengths influence how you teach. Try to match your strengths with each child's learning style needs. If

True Stories from the Trenches

I started out as a spiritually single mom and ended up a completely single mom. Through those years I thought there was little I could do to train my kids. After all, I had no emotional support from anyone. I certainly couldn't do after-dinner devotions. Nor could I take evenings for family activities with a spiritual emphasis. But there are more ways to impart faith lessons than just devotions, and more opportunities for activities than just the evening.

Each night I prayed with the children as they lay in their beds. I had printed a verse on a 3x5 card and read the same verse every night for a week. After the verse, I sang hymns to them. These times were precious as we discussed all sorts of things there in the darkness of their rooms. We talked about how God viewed friendships and how to pray for our enemies. We talked about hurts and God's presence with us at all times—even in the hard times.

Trips around town in the car afforded many opportunities to talk about how God views us, loves us, and wants us to act and care for others.

Our poverty provided faith lessons as we prayed for our needs and watched God miraculously answer those needs some of the time; at others He simply sustained us as we struggled.

Yes, such lessons took two of us—me and God.   —L. H. J.[3]

you are married, perhaps your spouse has a different personality type and can teach a particular child more effectively. If
you parent alone, use a variety of approaches. And no matter
what your situation may be, remember the word *grace*. God
will help you, so be patient with yourself!

Looking Back

Now that we have completed our last session
together, what stands out as you think about
everything we have read and discussed? Why is it so important for us to start using what we've learned with our children instead of waiting until we'll have more time or energy
or money or less stress? What are some of the temptations
that will arise and try to derail our family spiritual growth
plans?

Just Try It!

✹ **Twelve Spy** *(no time limit, all ages)*

As you ride in a car, mention that there were 12 tribes of Israel and 12 disciples of Jesus. Then decide on which object you and your children will find first. The first person who sees 12 of that particular object wins.

For example, maybe you choose red pickup trucks as your object for one round of this game. After the word "Go!" everyone will quietly count red pickup trucks until someone gets to 12 and says, "Twelve spy."

To continue playing, pick a new object (buses, food trucks, hotel signs, etc.), and start again.

Give one point to each participant. Give an additional point to the winner of each round.[4]

✹ **Bedtime Blessing: "Water Trombone"** *(ages 6 and under)*

Materials needed: empty soda bottle and a drinking straw. (Before you start tonight's experiment, fill the soda bottle about three-quarters full of water.)

Say: "Tonight we will be making a water trombone."

Do: Put the straw in the bottle and blow across the top of the straw. Then let your child take a turn.

Say: "A real trombone is also called a slide trombone because you change the tone by sliding part of the instrument up and down. We can do the same thing with our water trombone."

Do: Hold the bottle in your hand and the straw in the other. Now move the bottle up and down as you are blowing across the straw. Then give the instrument to your child.

Say: "What happens to the sound when you lower the bottle?" (The sound will drop to a lower pitch.)

Say: "What do you think will happen when you lift the bottle?" *(Have your child predict what will happen, then test his or her predictions. Let your child experiment with some tunes before you say your prayers.)*

Pray: "Dear God, Thank You for music, and for the joy it brings. Help our lives to be like music to other people's ears so that we can bring a little joy into their lives, too. Thank You for the joy that _____ [child's name] brings me. Amen."[5]

✳ Special Blend

Materials needed: A different color of paint for each family member, toothpicks to dip into the paint, sheet of white paper, and a Bible.

Say: "Today the life slogan for this Family Night is, 'God so loved me, He made my family.' "

Do: Give each person a different color of paint and a toothpick. Begin with the color you have. Let one drop of your color drip onto the sheet of white paper, being careful that the paint doesn't bleed through. If you are married, then have your spouse let one drop of his or her color drip into your drop. If not, select another family member such as a child to do this. After your spouse (or other family member) drips the drop of paint, share one good quality that he or she brings to your family. For example, "Sharon brings enthusiasm to our family" or "Bill brings a listening ear to our family." If you like, let all the family members share something positive they think this person adds to the family.

Use a toothpick to mix these colors together.

Then have each additional child add a drop of his or her color, mixing in each new addition of paint. Each time, continue to share a good quality about each child, such as "Allison adds laughter to our family" or "Taylor has a helpful attitude." Do this until all family members have had the chance to add their individual colors.

Ask: "What new color was created? Can we ever go back to the original colors? Why or why not?"

Say: "God made our family unlike any other family. Even if another family has the same number of children as ours, or lives in an apartment or house like ours, or even has our names, no other family is like ours. We're a special blend of people that God has put together! We each have different interests, and we each have special roles in our family. Each of us is special, and together we make a one-of-a-kind family!"[6]

Discussion Questions

The following questions are designed to stimulate discussion in a small-group setting such as a neighborhood Bible study, Sunday school class, or parenting class. We encourage you to listen to the audiotape for each session as a group before discussing the questions, but you may choose to use only this book if your group time is quite limited. It would be best if everyone in your group has the book and is excited about using it with their children.

Let's Talk About It
- How important is it for us to creatively match elements of our families' spiritual growth plan to our children's interests and personalities? Why?
- What can happen if we act as if all our children have the same type of personality, such as that of a Lion or an Otter, but all their personalities are different?
- Which issues may crop up if a parent is a Lion and his or her child is a Beaver? Why?

APPENDIX

How to Lead Your Child to Christ

SOME THINGS TO CONSIDER AHEAD OF TIME

1. Realize that God is more concerned about your child's eternal destiny and happiness than you are. "The Lord is not slow in keeping his promise.... He is patient with you, not wanting anyone to perish, but everyone to come to repentance" (2 Peter 3:9).
2. Pray specifically beforehand that God will give you insights and wisdom in dealing with each child on his or her maturity level.
3. Don't use terms like "take Jesus into your heart," "dying and going to hell," and "accepting Christ as your personal Savior." Children are either too literal ("How does Jesus breathe in my heart?") or the words are too clichéd and trite for their understanding.
4. Deal with each child alone, and don't be in a hurry. Make sure he or she understands. Discuss. Take your time.

A FEW CAUTIONS

1. When drawing children to Himself, Jesus said for others to "let" them to come to Him (see Mark 10:14). Only with

adults did He use the term "make" (see Luke 14:23). Do not *make* children.

2. Remember that unless the Holy Spirit is speaking to the child, there will be no genuine heart experience of regeneration. Parents, don't get caught up in the idea that Jesus will return the day before you were going to speak to your child about salvation and that it will be too late. Look at God's character—He *is* love! He is not dangling your child's soul over hell. Wait on God's timing. Pray with faith, believing. Be concerned, but don't push.

The Plan

1. **God loves you.** Recite John 3:16, explaining that "the world" means all people, including the child.
2. **Show the need of a Savior.**
   a. Deal with sin carefully. There is one thing that cannot enter heaven—sin.
   b. Be sure your child knows what sin is. Ask him to name some (things common to children—lying, sassing, disobeying, etc.). Sin is doing or thinking anything wrong according to God's Word. It is breaking God's Law.
   c. Ask the question "Have you sinned?" If the answer is no, do not continue. Urge him to come and talk to you again when he does feel that he has sinned. Dismiss him. You may want to have prayer first, however, thanking God "for this young child who is willing to do what is right." Make it easy for him to talk to you again but do not continue. Do not say, "Oh, yes you have too sinned!" and then name some. With children, wait for God's conviction.
   d. If the answer is yes, continue. He may even give a personal illustration of some sin he has done recently or one that has bothered him.
   e. Tell him what God says about sin: We've all sinned ("There is no one righteous, not even one," Rom. 3:10). And because of that sin, we can't get to God ("For the

wages of sin is death . . ." Rom. 6:23). So He had to come to us (". . . but the gift of God is eternal life in Christ Jesus our Lord," Rom. 6:23).

   f. Related God's gift of salvation to Christmas gifts—we don't earn them or pay for them; we just accept them and are thankful for them.

3. **Bring the child to a definite decision.**
   a. Christ must be received if salvation is to be possessed.
   b. Remember, do not force a decision.
   c. Ask the child to pray out loud in her own words. Give her some things she could say if she seems unsure. Now be prepared for a blessing! (It is best to avoid having the child repeat a memorized prayer after you. Let her think, and make it personal.)*
   d. After salvation has occurred, pray for her out loud. This is a good way to pronounce a blessing on her.

4. **Lead your child into assurance.**
Show him that he will have to keep his relationship open with God through repentance and forgiveness (just like with his family or friends), but that God will always love him ("Never will I leave you; never will I forsake you," Heb. 13:5).

* If you wish to guide your child through the prayer, here is some suggested language.

> *"Dear God, I know that I am a sinner [have child name specific sins he or she acknowledged earlier, such as lying, stealing, disobeying, etc.]. I know that Jesus died on the cross to pay for all my sins. I ask You to forgive me of my sins. I believe that Jesus died for me and rose from the dead, and I accept Him as my Savior. Thank You for loving me. In Jesus' name, Amen."*

Notes

Session 1:

1. Adapted from *Focus on the Family's Parents' Guide to the Spiritual Growth of Children*, eds. John Trent, Ph.D., Rick Osborne, and Kurt Bruner (Wheaton, Ill.: Tyndale House, 2000), pp. 1-2.
2. *Parents' Guide*, p. 27.
3. *Parents' Guide*, pp. 17-19.

Session 2:

1. Adapted from *Focus on the Family's Parents' Guide to the Spiritual Growth of Children*, eds. John Trent, Ph.D., Rick Osborne, and Kurt Bruner (Wheaton, Ill.: Tyndale House, 2000), p. 23.
2. Greg Johnson and Mike Yorkey, *Faithful Parents, Faithful Kids* (Wheaton, Ill.: Tyndale House, 1993).
3. For more information, read Josh McDowell's book *Right from Wrong* (Dallas: Word, 1994).
4. *Parents' Guide*, p. 25.
5. *Parents' Guide*, p. 28.
6. *Parents' Guide*, p. 30.
7. *Parents' Guide*, p. 32.
8. *Parents' Guide*, p. 34.
9. Adapted from *Family Nights Tool Chest: Bible Stories for Preschoolers (New Testament)*, by Kirk Weaver, Jim Weidmann, and Kurt Bruner (Colorado Springs, Colo.: Chariot Victor, 1996), pp. 17-18.
10. Adapted from *Mealtime Moments: 164 Faith-Filling Entrees to Stir Family Discussion*, by Crystal Bowman and Tricia Goyer (Wheaton, Ill.: Tyndale House, 2000), p. 87.

Session 3:

1. Adapted from *Your Heritage: How to Be Intentional About the Legacy You Leave,* by J. Otis Ledbetter and Kurt Bruner (Colorado Springs, Colo.: Cook Communications, 1996), p. 54.
2. *Parents' Guide,* p. 44.
3. *Parents' Guide,* pp. 33-34.
4. From *Family Nights Tool Chest: Christian Character Qualities,* by Jim Weidmann and Kurt Bruner, with Mike & Amy Nappa (Colorado Springs, Colo.: Cook Communications, 1998), pp. 63-64.

Session 4:

1. *Family Fragrance: Practical, Intentional Ways to Fill Your Home with the Aroma of Love,* by J. Otis & Gail Ledbetter (Colorado Springs, Colo.: Cook Communications, 1998), p. 25.
2. *Family Fragrance,* p. 30.
3. *Family Fragrance,* p. 41.
4. *Family Fragrance,* p. 41.
5. *Family Fragrance,* p. 60.
6. Adapted from *Family Fragrance,* p. 103.
7. *Family Fragrance,* p. 87.
8. Adapted from *Family Fragrance,* p. 104.
9. Adapted from *Family Fragrance,* pp. 139–141.
10. *Family Fragrance,* p. 146.
11. Adapted from *Family Fragrance,* p. 119.
12. *Mealtime Moments: 164 Faith-Filling Entrees to Stir Family Discussion,* by Crystal Bowman and Tricia Goyer (Wheaton, Ill.: Tyndale House, 2000), p. 166.

Session 5:

1. *Family Traditions,* by J. Otis Ledbetter and Tim Smith (Colorado Springs, Colo.: Chariot Victor, 1999), p. 32.
2. To learn more about how to give the gift of blessing, see chapter 24 of *Focus on the Family's Parents' Guide to the Spiritual Growth of Children.*

3. *The Family Compass: Practical, Intentional Ways to Pass Godly Values on to Your Child,* by Kurt & Olivia Bruner (Colorado Springs, Colo.: Chariot Victor, 1999), p. 48.

4. *The Family Compass,* p. 54.

5. Research provided by Barna Research Online, www.barna.org. Used by permission.

6. *Family Traditions,* p. 46.

7. Adapted from *The Family Compass,* p. 44.

8. Adapted from "Run for Your Life" in *Joy Ride! Faith-Filled Fun & Games for Drivetime,* by Jacqueline Lederman (Wheaton, Ill.: Tyndale House, 2000), p. 39.

9. Adapted from "The Most Important Commandment" in *Bedtime Blessings,* by John Trent, Ph.D. (Wheaton, Ill.: Tyndale House, 2000), p. 138.

Session 6:

1. You can find a similar version of this chart on the Heritage Builders Web site: www.heritagebuilders.com

2. Adapted from *Focus on the Family's Parents' Guide to the Spiritual Growth of Children,* eds. John Trent, Ph.D., Rick Osborne, and Kurt Bruner (Wheaton, Ill.: Tyndale House, 2000), p. 156.

3. *Parents' Guide,* p. 41.

4. Adapted from "Twelve Spy" in *Joy Ride! Faith-Filled Fun & Games for Drivetime,* by Jacqueline Lederman (Wheaton, Ill.: Tyndale House, 2000), p. 20.

5. Adapted from "Let's Do an Experiment: Water Trombone" in *Bedtime Blessings,* by John Trent, Ph.D. (Wheaton, Ill.: Tyndale House, 2000), p. 86.

6. Adapted from *Family Nights Tool Chest: Basic Christian Beliefs,* by Jim Weidmann and Kurt Bruner (Colorado Springs, Colo.: Cook Communications, 1998), pp. 105, 109-110.

Welcome to the Family!

Heritage Builders

Helping You Build a Family of Faith

We hope you've enjoyed this book. Heritage Builders was founded in 1995 by three fathers with a passion for the next generation. As a new ministry of Focus on the Family, Heritage Builders strives to equip, train, and motivate parents to become intentional about building a strong spiritual heritage.

It's quite a challenge for busy parents to find ways to build a spiritual foundation for their families—especially in a way they enjoy and understand. Through activities and participation, children can learn biblical truth in a way they can understand, enjoy—and *remember.*

Passing along a heritage of Christian faith to your family is a parent's highest calling. Heritage Builders' goal is to encourage and empower you in this great mission with practical resources and inspiring ideas that really work—and help your children develop a lasting love for God.

***

How to Reach Us

For more information, visit our Heritage Builders Web site! Log on to **www.heritagebuilders.com** to discover new resources, sample activities, and ideas to help you pass on a spiritual heritage. To request any of these resources, simply call Focus on the Family at 1-800-A-FAMILY (1-800-232-6459) or in Canada, call 1-800-661-9800. Or send your request to Focus on the Family, Colorado Springs, CO 80995. In Canada, write Focus on the Family, P.O. Box 9800, Stn. Terminal, Vancouver, B.C. V6B 4G3.

To learn more about Focus on the Family or to find out if there is an associate office in your country, please visit www.family.org.

We'd love to hear from you!

Try These Heritage Builders Resources!

Parents' Guide to the Spiritual Growth of Children

Passing on a foundation of faith to your child is an awesome responsibility. Now, the job is easier with *Parents' Guide to the Spiritual Growth of Children,* co-edited by best-selling author John Trent, Rick Osborne, and Kurt Bruner. Simple, practical and comprehensive, it's a terrific tool for developing your child's Christian values from birth to age 12. Filled with answers to the questions parents ask most, it's a reassuring guide that helps you make sure your child is progressing spiritually.

An Introduction to Family Nights Tool Chest

Got a tube of toothpaste and a Bible? You've got all you need for a fun-filled night of values training. Part of the "Family Nights Tool Chest" series, *An Introduction to Family Nights Tool Chest,* delivers 12 weeks of tried-and-tested ideas and activities for helping kids learn how to tame the tongue, resist temptation, obey, and much more! If you want a spiritually strong family—and who doesn't?—grab the kids, head for the family room, and make play times the means for creating a godly heritage.

Bedtime Blessings

Strengthen the bond between you and your child by making *Bedtime Blessings* a special part of your evenings together. From best-selling author John Trent, Ph.D., this book offers countless ways to reaffirm the love God has for your child. Designed for children ages seven and under, it's a wonderful way to develop a habit of speaking encouraging words and blessing just before your son or daughter goes to sleep.

Mealtime Moments

Make your family's time around the dinner table meaningful with *Mealtime Moments.* This book brings you great discussion starters and activities to help you grow spiritually as well as grow closer as a family. Featuring theme nights, trivia, daily Bible verses, prayers, interesting discussion topics and more, your children will be learning terrific biblical principles in fun, memorable ways. Each lesson provides a well-balanced diet of spiritually sound ideas that are easy to work into your daily mealtime—helping you build a solid heritage of faith for the whole family.

Joy Ride!

When you think of all the time kids spend in the car, it makes sense to use the time to teach lasting spiritual lessons along the way. *Joy Ride!* is a fun and challenging activity book that helps parents blend biblical principles into everyday life. Games, puzzles, Bible-quiz questions, and discussion starters give parents fun ways to get the whole family involved in talking and thinking about their faith. Make the most of your time together on the road with this fun, inspiring guide. Small enough to fit into a glove compartment, it's great for vacations and local trips!

Heritage
Builders
Helping You Build a Family of Faith

Every family has a heritage—a spiritual, emotional, and social legacy passed from one generation to the next. There are four main areas we at Heritage Builders recommend parents consider as they plan to pass their faith to their children:

Family Fragrance
Every family's home has a fragrance. Heritage Builders encourages parents to create a home environment that fosters a sweet, Christ-centered AROMA of love through Affection, Respect, Order, Merriment, and Affirmation.

Family Traditions
Whether you pass down stories, beliefs, and/or customs, traditions can help you establish a special identity for your family. Heritage Builders encourages parents to set special "milestones" for their children to help guide them and move them through their spiritual development.

Family Compass
Parents have the unique task of setting standards for normal, healthy living through their attitudes, actions, and beliefs. Heritage Builders encourages parents to give their children the moral navigation tools they need to succeed on the roads of life.

Family Moments
Creating special, teachable moments with their children is one of a parent's most precious, and sometimes most difficult, responsibilities. Heritage Builders encourages parents to capture little moments throughout the day to teach and impress values, beliefs, and biblical principles onto their children.

We look forward to standing alongside you as you seek to impart the Lord's care and wisdom to the next generation—to your children.

Heritage Builders®
Helping You Build a Family of Faith